W9-ANJ-701

GUITAR HERO

™

Artwork © Activision

ISBN 13: 978-1-4234-4692-7
ISBN 10: 1-4234-4692-5

HAL•LEONARD® CORPORATION

7777 W. BLUEMOUND RD. P.O. BOX 13819 MILWAUKEE, WI 53213

Visit Hal Leonard Online at
www.halleonard.com

Bark at the Moon

Words and Music by Ozzy Osbourne

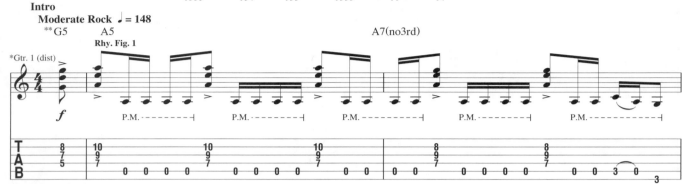

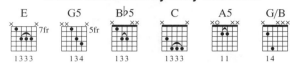

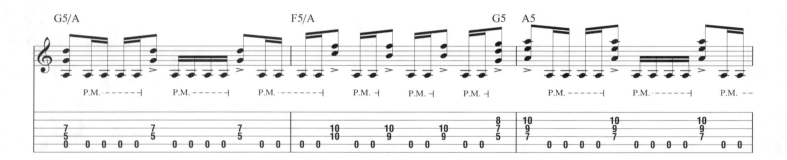

*Two gtrs. arr. for one
**Chord symbols reflect basic harmony.

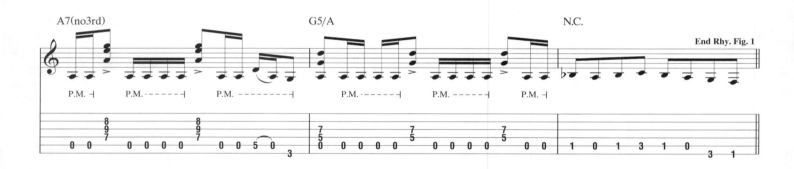

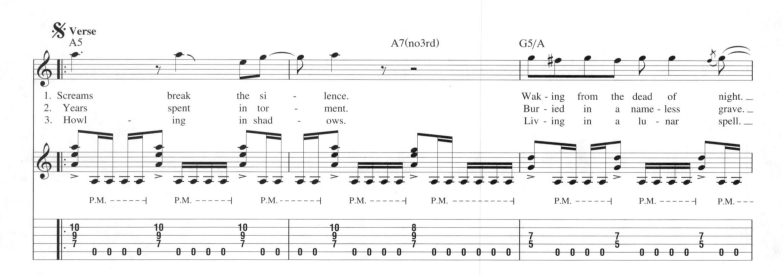

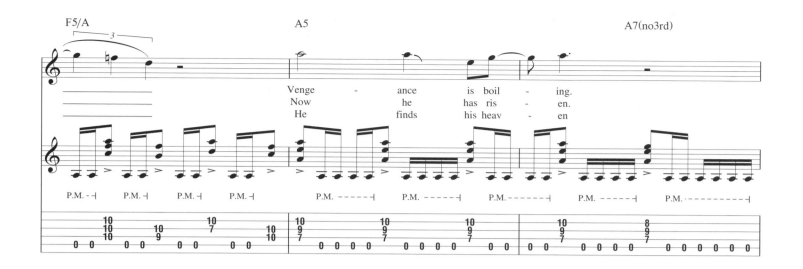

Venge - ance is boil - ing.
Now he has ris - en.
He finds his heav - en

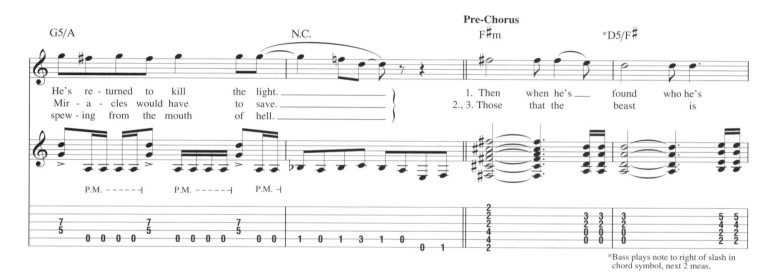

He's re - turned to kill the light.
Mir - a - cles would have to save.
spew - ing from the mouth of hell.

1. Then when he's found who he's
2., 3. Those that the beast is

*Bass plays note to right of slash in chord symbol, next 2 meas.

2nd time, Gtr. 1: w/ Fill 2
3rd time, Gtr. 1: w/ Fill 3

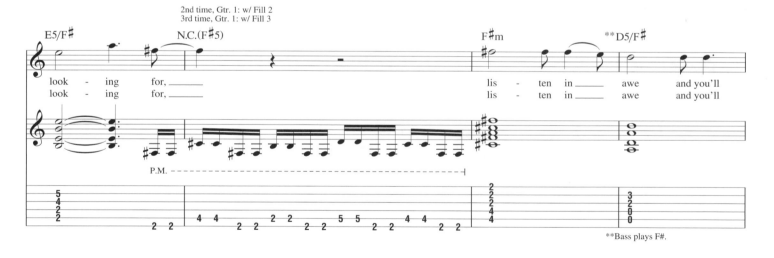

look - ing for, lis - ten in awe and you'll
look - ing for, lis - ten in awe and you'll

**Bass plays F#.

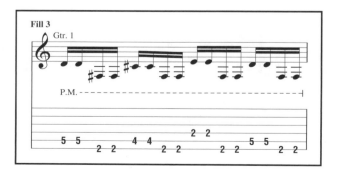

5

Bridge
Half-time feel

They cursed and bur-ied him, a-long with ____ shame.

*Gtrs. 1 & 2
Rhy. Fig. 3

*Composite arrangement; starts on beat 4 1/2 before Bridge.

And thought his time-less soul had gone, ____ gone. ____

End Rhy. Fig. 3

Gtrs. 1 & 2: w/ Rhy. Fig. 3

In emp-ty burn-ing hell un-ho-ly ____ one. ____

But he's re-turned to prove them wrong, ____ so wrong. ____

Gtr. 2

Gtr. 1

let ring

Guitar Solo

End half-time feel

Ooh yeah, ba - by.

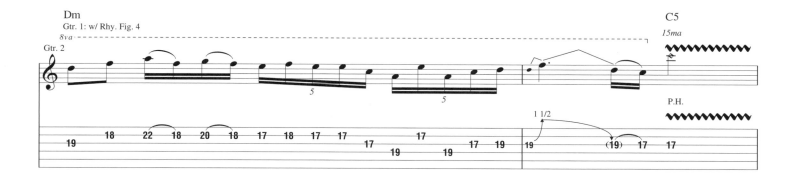

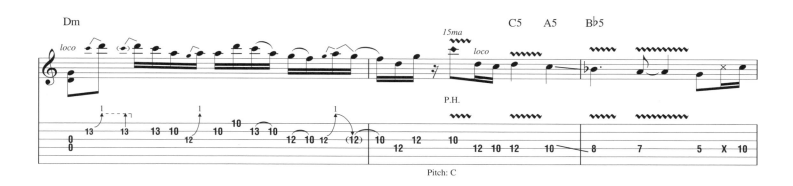

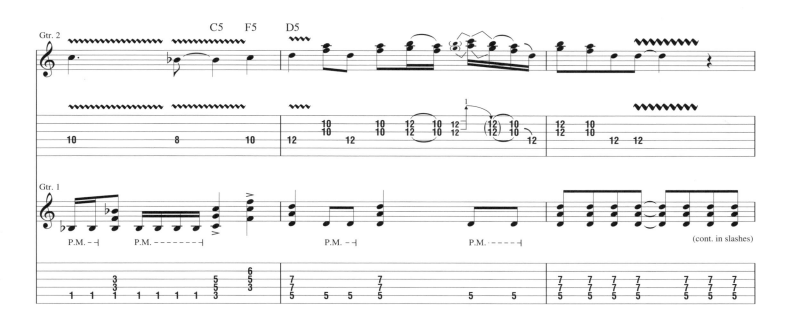

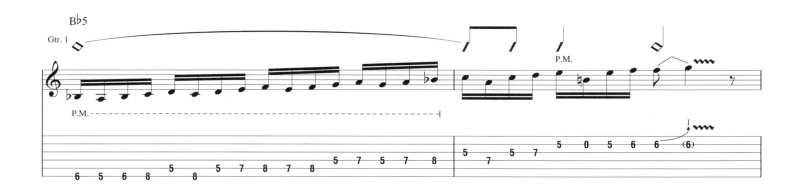

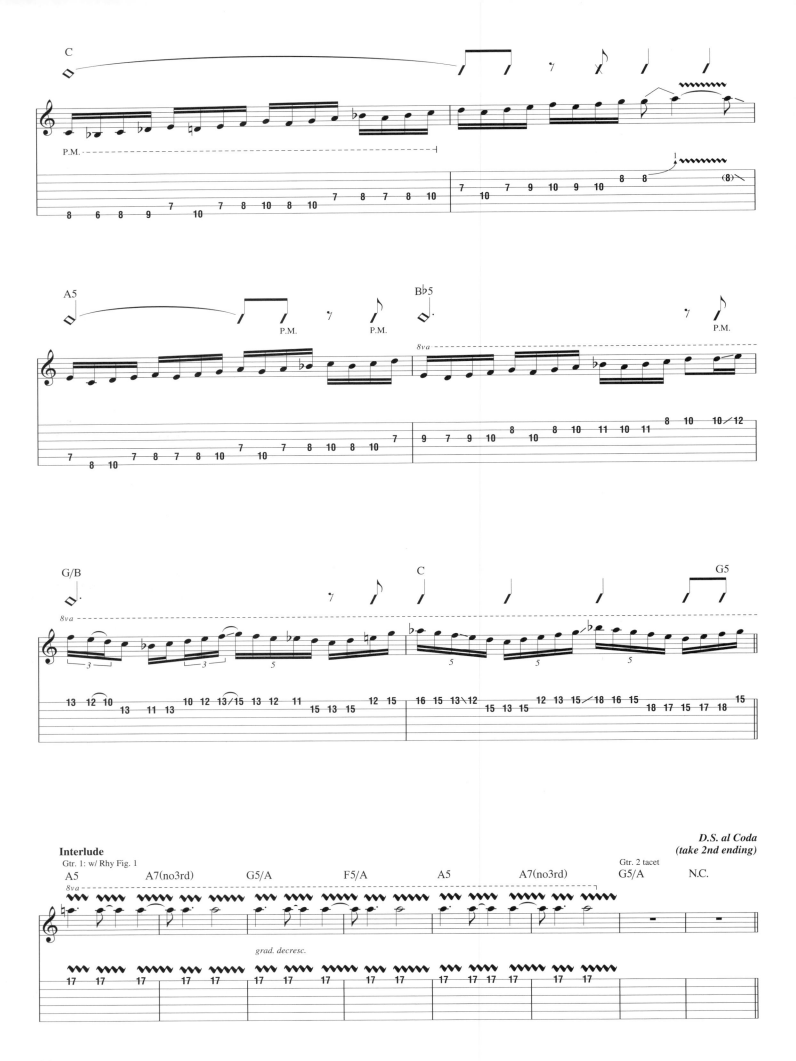

Beast and the Harlot

Words and Music by Matthew Sanders, James Sullivan, Brian Haner, Jr. and Zachary Baker

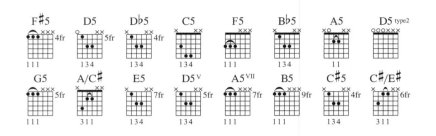

Drop D tuning:
(low to high) D-A-D-G-B-E

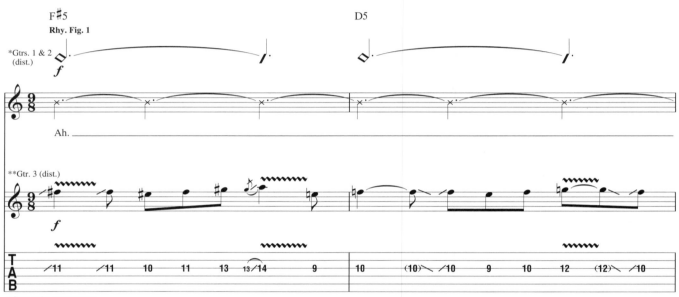

*Composite arrangement
**Two gtrs. arr. for one.

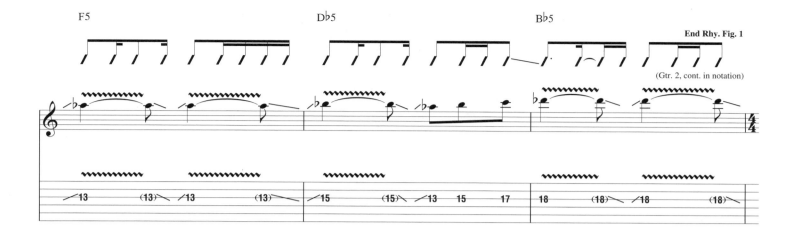

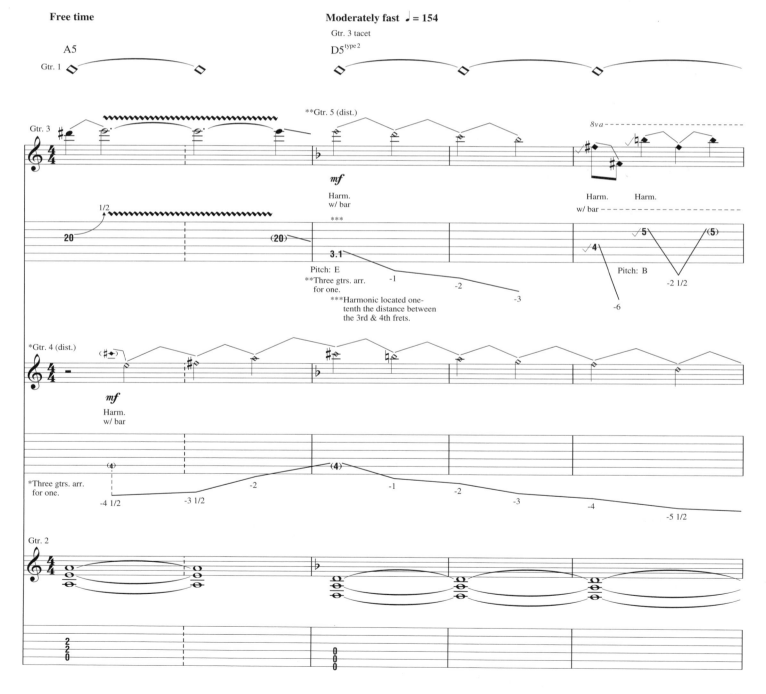

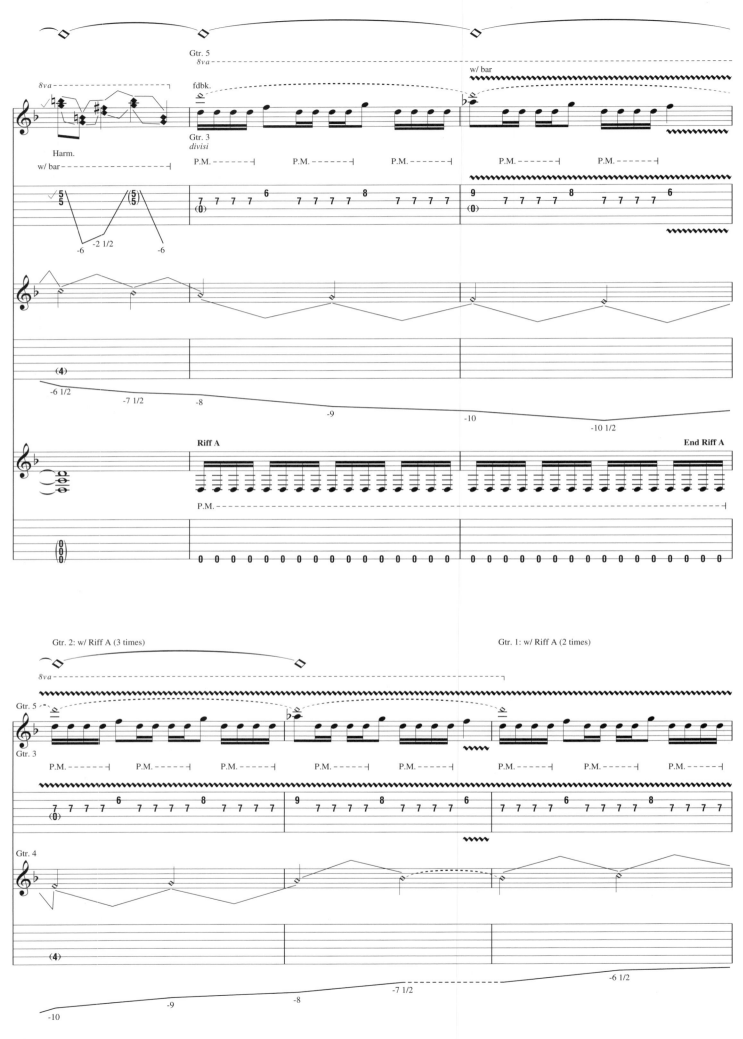

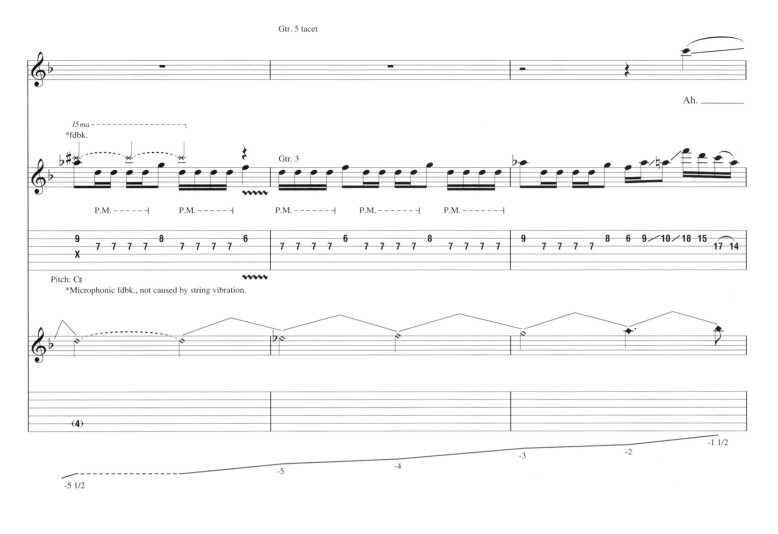

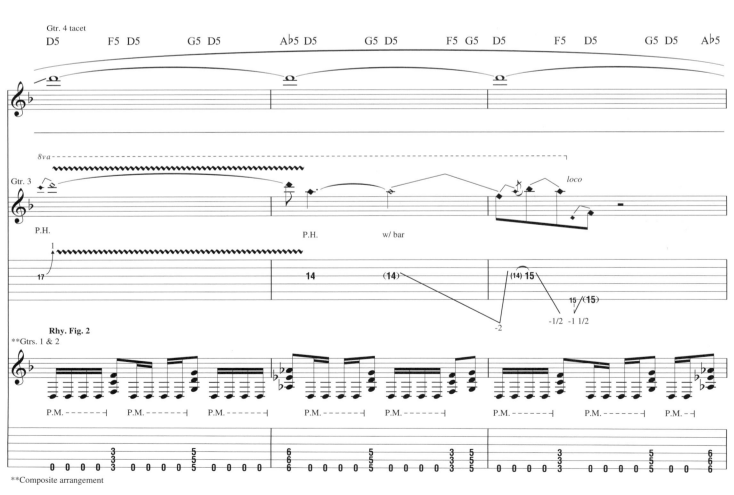

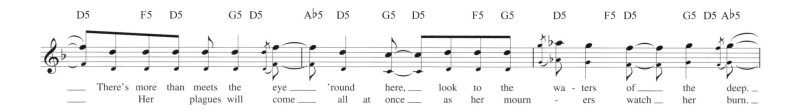

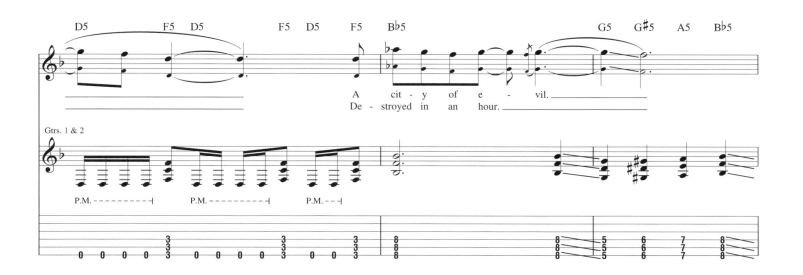

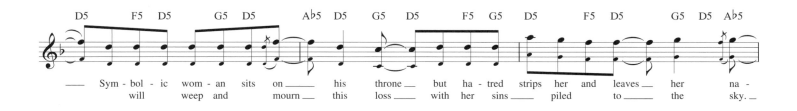

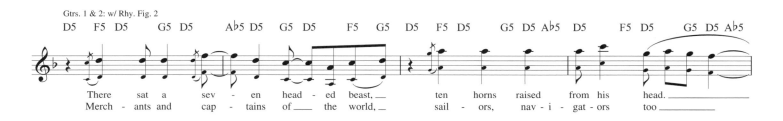

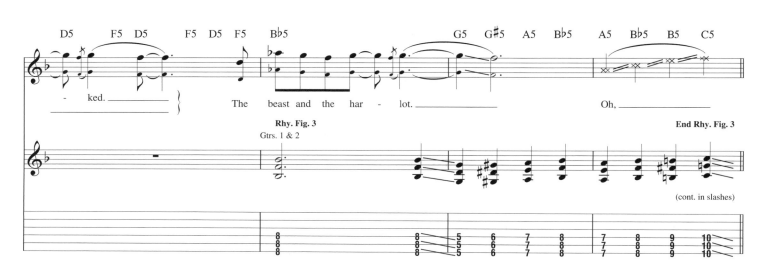

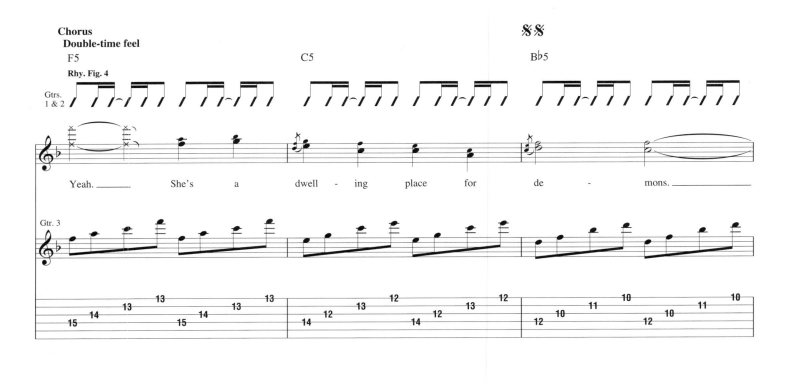

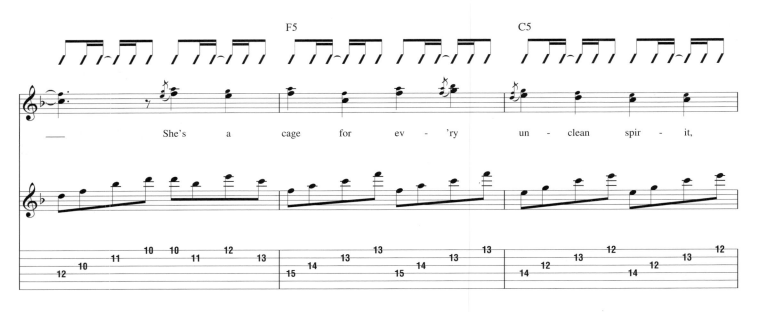

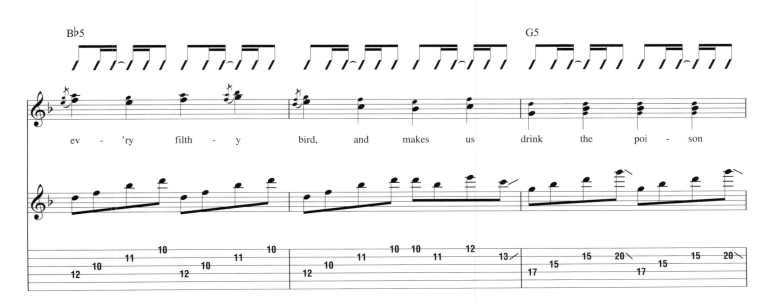

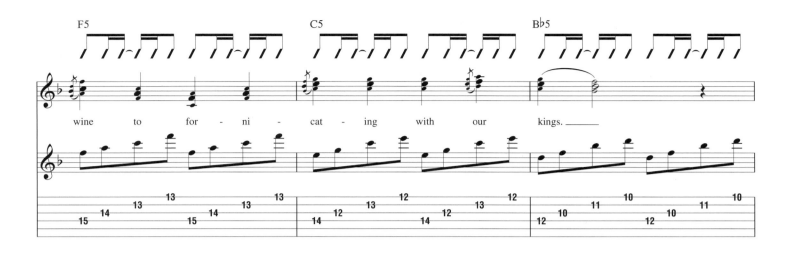

wine to for-ni-cat-ing with our kings. _____

To Coda 2 ⊕   To Coda 1 ⊕
                               End double-time feel
                               End Rhy. Fig. 4

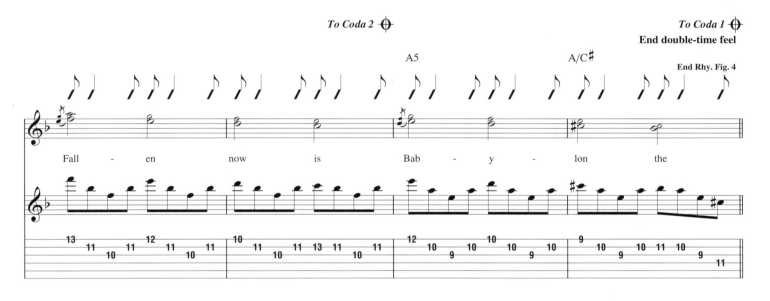

Fall-en now is Bab-y-lon the

Guitar Solo

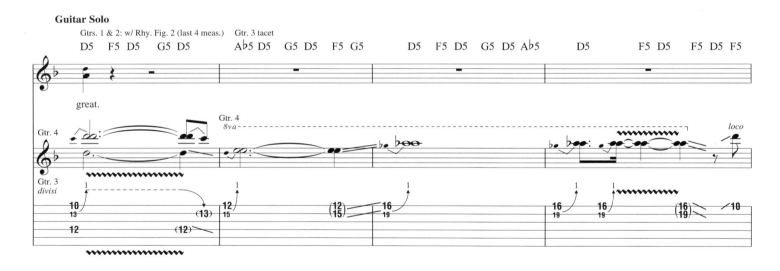

great.

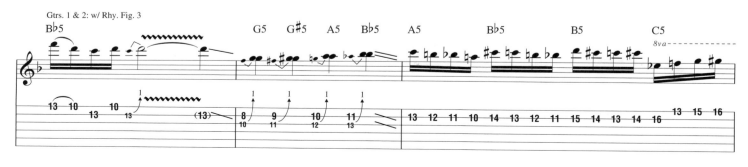

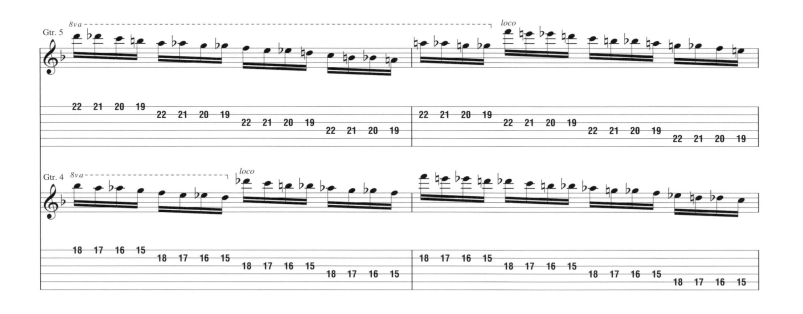

D.S. al Coda 1
End double-time feel

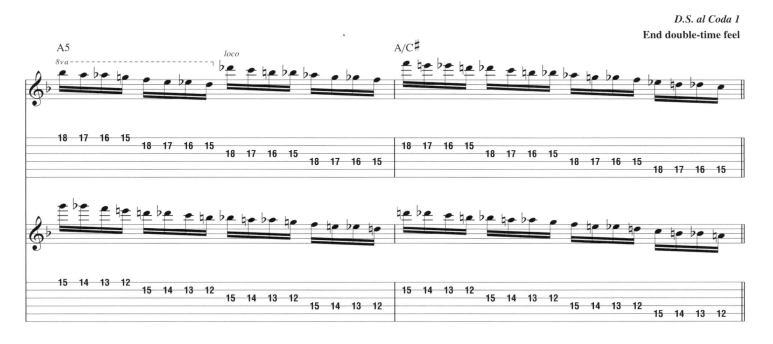

⊕ Coda 1

Interlude

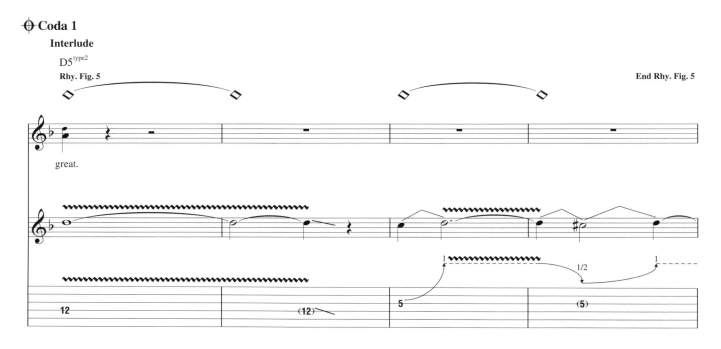

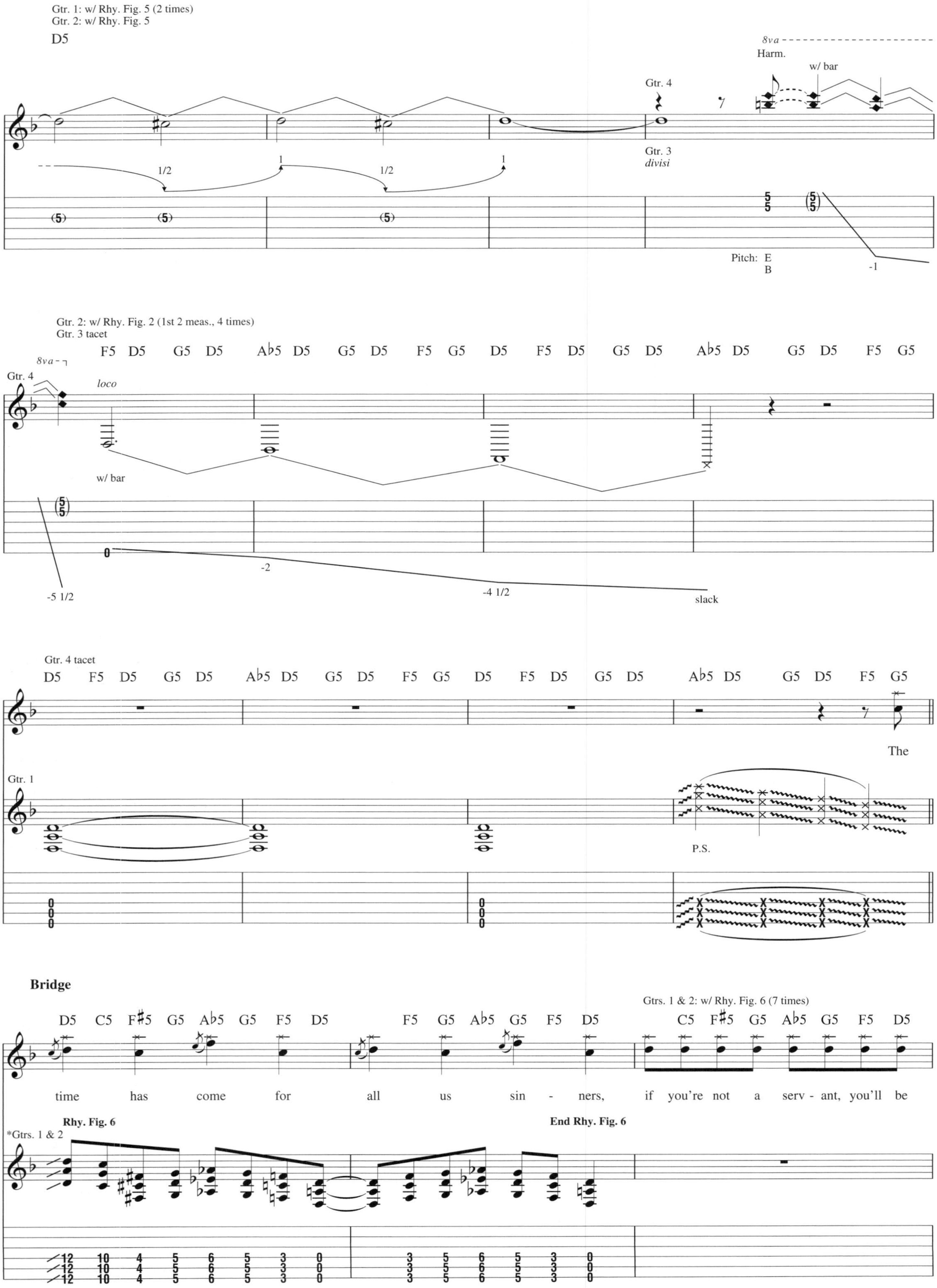

*Composite arrangement

struck to the ground. _____ Flee the burn - ing, greed - y cit - y,

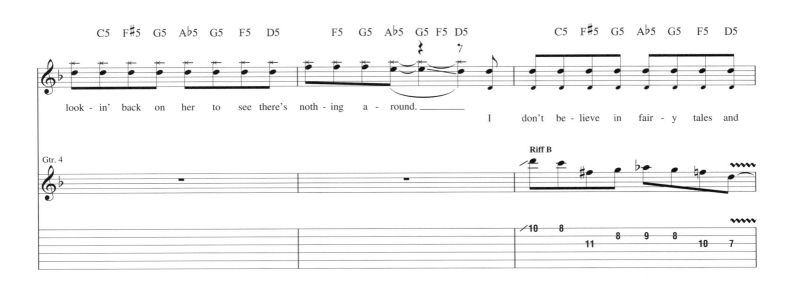

look - in' back on her to see there's noth - ing a - round. _____ I don't be - lieve in fair - y tales and

Riff B

no one wants to go to hell. We've made the wrong de - ci - sion and it's eas - y to see. _____ Now

End Riff B

Gtr. 4: w/ Riff B

if you wan - na serve a - bove or be a king be - low with us, you're wel - come to the cit - y where your

Gtr. 5

Coda 2

cage for ev - 'ry un - clean spir - it, ev - 'ry filth - y

bird, and makes us drink the poi - son wine to for - ni -

Outro

Gtrs. 1 & 2: w/ Rhy. Fig. 1

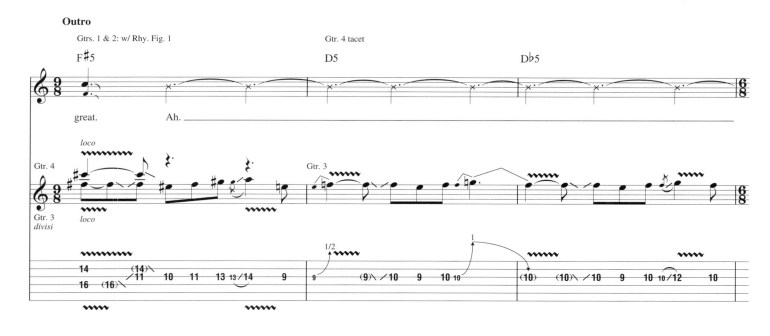

Gtr. 4 tacet

great.   Ah. _____

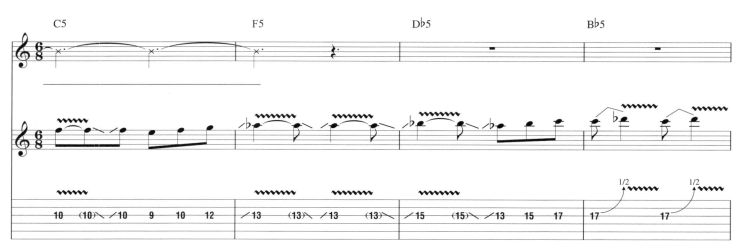

Segue to "Burn It Down"

Faster ♩ = 176

Gtr. 3 tacet

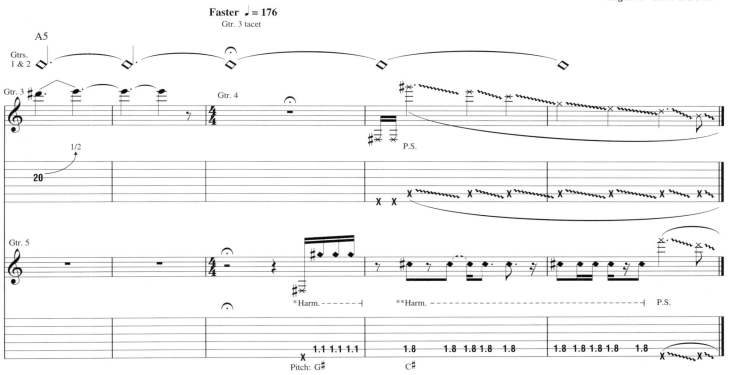

Pitch: G♯   C♯

*Harmonic located one-tenth the distance between the 2nd & 3rd frets.

**Harmonic located eight-tenths the distance between the 2nd & 3rd frets.

Carry On Wayward Son

Words and Music by Kerry Livgren

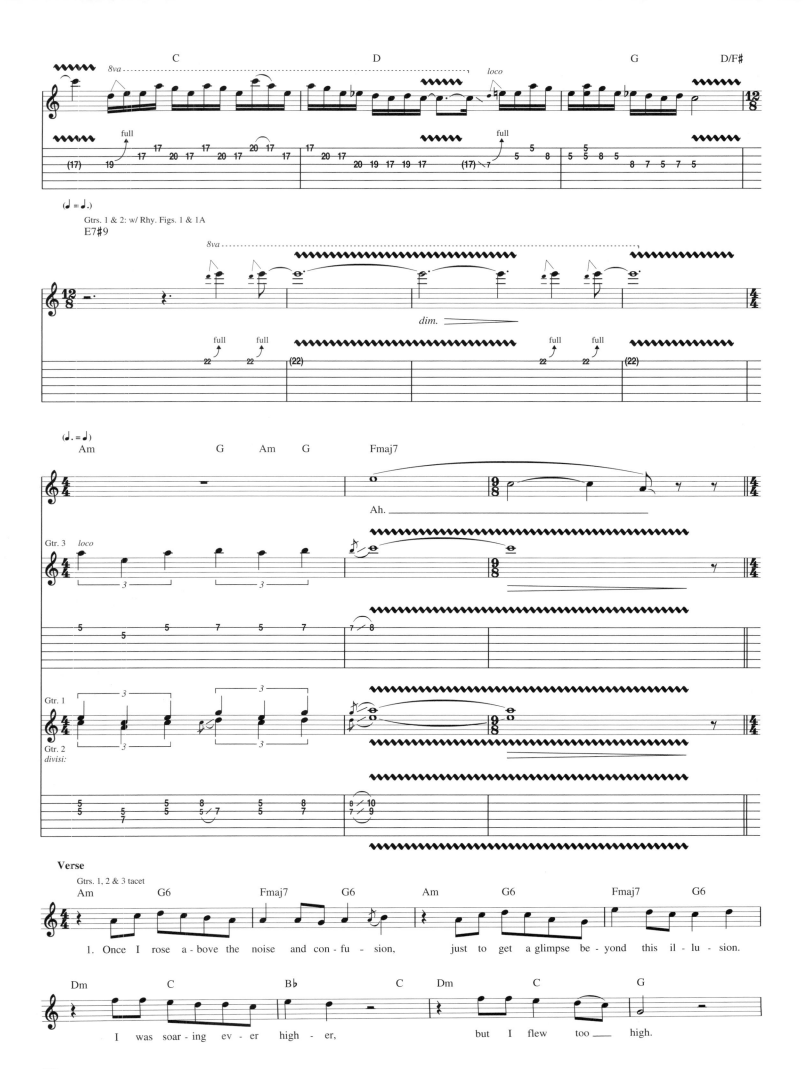

'Though my eyes could see, I still was a blind man. 'Though my mind could think, I still was a mad-man.

Gtr. 4 Rhy. Fig. 2
(acous.)

mf

let ring throughout

I hear the voi-ces when I'm dream-ing. I can hear them say:

End Rhy. Fig. 2

Chorus

Gtr. 4 tacet

"Car-ry on, my way-ward son,_____ There'll be peace when you___ are done.___

Gtr. 1 Rhy. Fig. 3

w/ clean tone

let ring throughout

Lay your wear-y head___ to rest._____ Don't you cry no___

End Rhy. Fig. 3

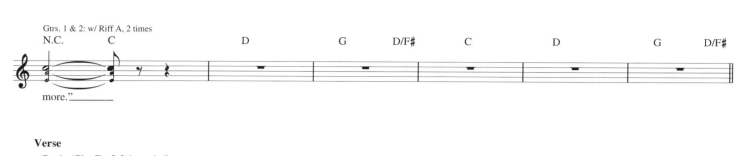

more."

Verse

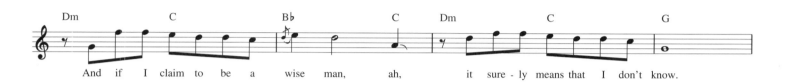

2. Mas-quer-ad-ing as a man with a rea-son. My cha-rade is the e-vent of the sea-son.

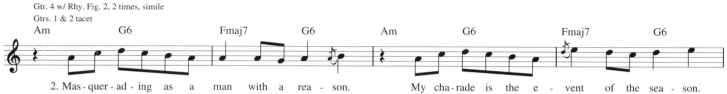

And if I claim to be a wise man, ah, it sure-ly means that I don't know.

On a storm-y sea of mov-ing e-mo-tion. Tossed a-bout, I'm like a ship on the o-cean.

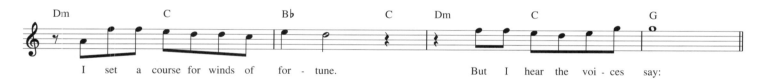

I set a course for winds of for-tune. But I hear the voi-ces say:

Chorus

"Car-ry on my way-ward son. There'll be peace when you ___ are done. ___

To Coda

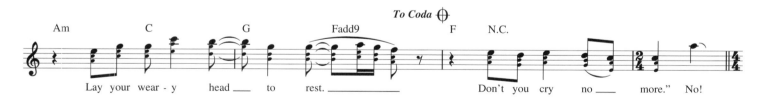

Lay your wear-y head ___ to rest. ___ Don't you cry no ___ more." No!

Interlude

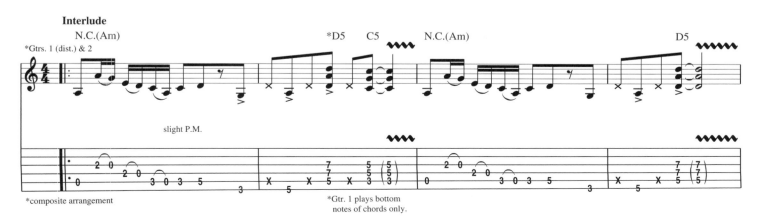

*composite arrangement

*Gtr. 1 plays bottom notes of chords only.

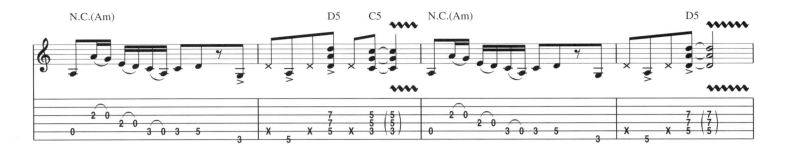

N.C.(Am)　　　　　　　　　　　　D5　C5　　　N.C.(Am)　　　　　　　　　　　D5

1.

Organ Solo

N.C.

Riff B　　　　　　　　　　　　　　　　　　　　　　　　　　　　　End Riff B

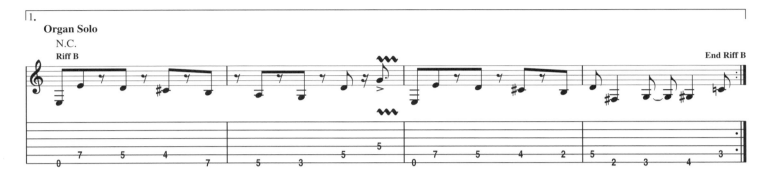

2.

Guitar Solo

Gtrs. 1 & 2: w/ Riff B

8va - *loco*

Gtr. 3

f

full

P.H.　　　　　　　P.H.　　P.H.　　　　P.H.

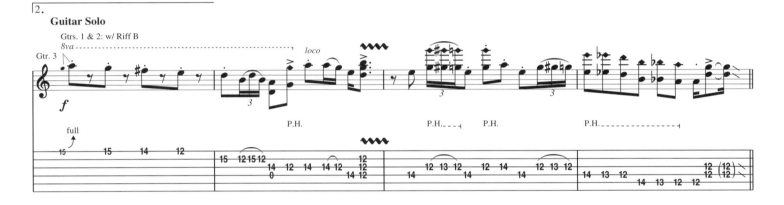

Interlude

Gtr. 3 tacet

Gtrs.　N.C.　　　　　　　　　C　　　　　　　D　　　　　　　　　　　G　　　D/F#
1 & 2

f

Bridge

A5　N.C.　　G5　F5　N.C.　　　　　A5　N.C.　　G5　F5　N.C.

Car - ry on,　you will　al - ways re - mem - ber. ___　　Car - ry on,　noth-ing　e - quals the splen - dor.

Gtr. 1　　　　　　　　　　Gtrs. 1 & 2　　　　　　　　Gtr. 1

Gtr. 2　　　　　　　　　　　　　　　Gtr. 2
divisi　　　　　　　　　　　　　　　　*divisi*

*　　　　　　　　　　　*

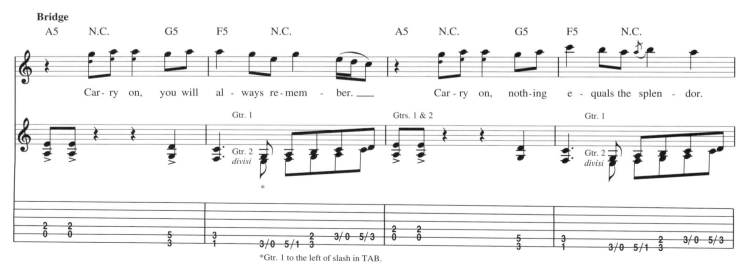

*Gtr. 1 to the left of slash in TAB.

Cherry Pie

Words and Music by Jani Lane

N.C.   C5   D5

I'm a trained pro - fes - sion - al.

Verse
Gtrs. 1 & 2: w/ Rhy. Figs. 3 & 3A   Gtr. 3 tacet
E5   D5   A

4. Swing - in' in the bath - room, swing - in' on the floor, swing - in' so hard, __ for - got to lock the door. __

Gtr. 3

E5

In   walk her dad - dy stand - in' six   foot   four,   said, "You ain't gon - na swing with my daugh - ter no   more."

Gtr. 2

Gtr. 1

Crazy on You

Words and Music by Ann Wilson, Nancy Wilson and Roger Fisher

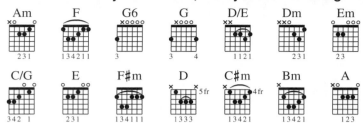

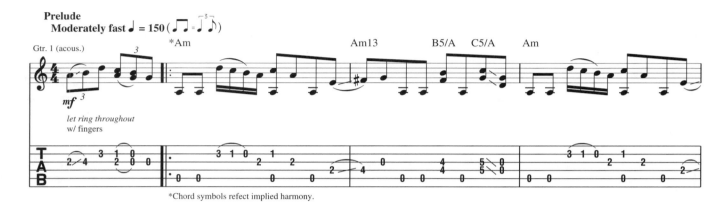

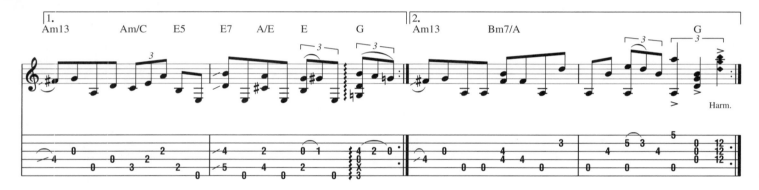

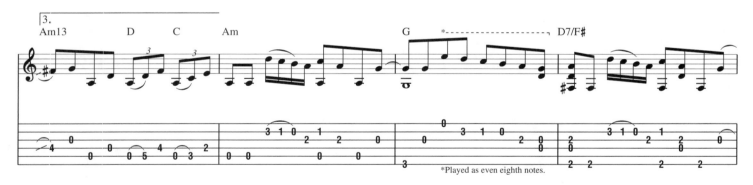

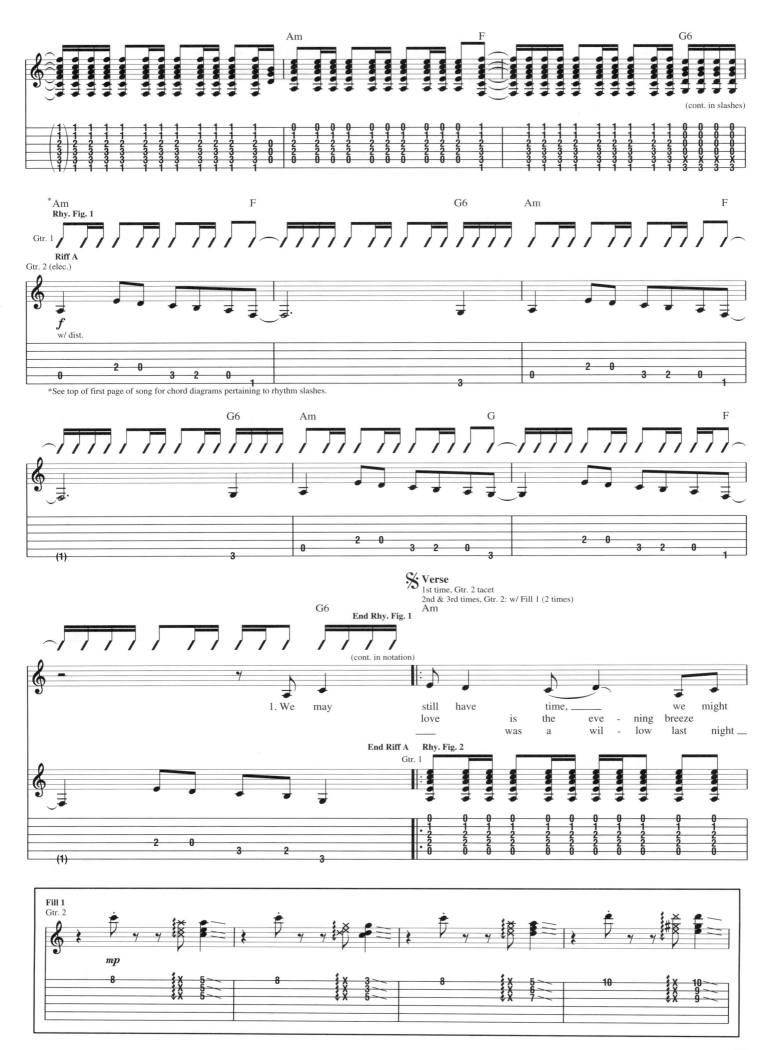

*Refers to downstemmed voc. only.

Outro-Chorus

Gtr. 1: w/ Rhy. Fig. 1 (1st 6 meas.)
Gtr. 2: w/ Riff A (1st 6 meas.)

Am   F   G6   Am   F   G6

Cra - zy on you,   cra - zy on ___ you. ___   Let me go

Gtr. 1: w/ *Rhy. Fill 1
Gtr. 2: w/ *Fill 2

Am   G   F   Am

cra - zy, cra - zy on you, _____ oh. ___

* Last meas. w/ fermata.

Cross Road Blues
(Crossroads)
Words and Music by Robert Johnson

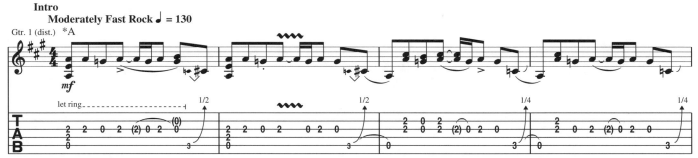

*Chord symbols reflect overall tonality throughout.

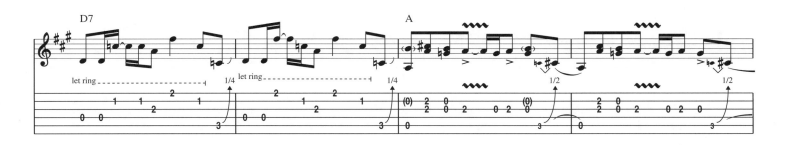

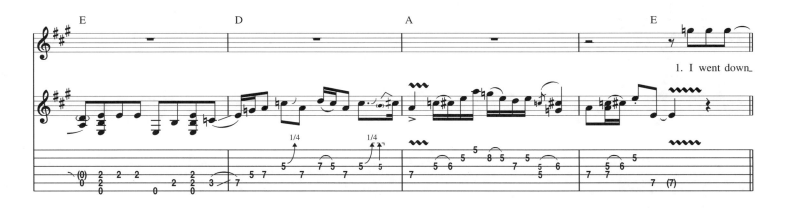

Frankenstein

By Edgar Winter

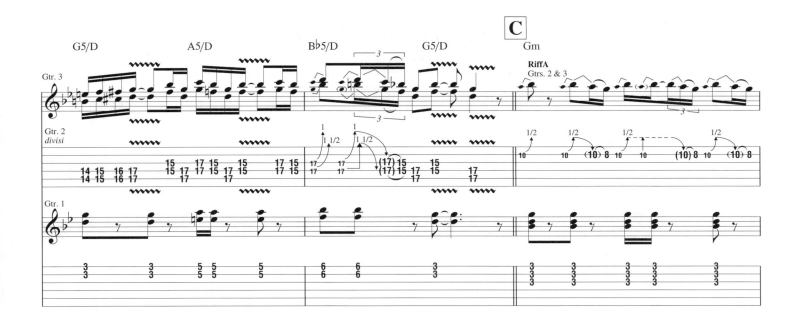

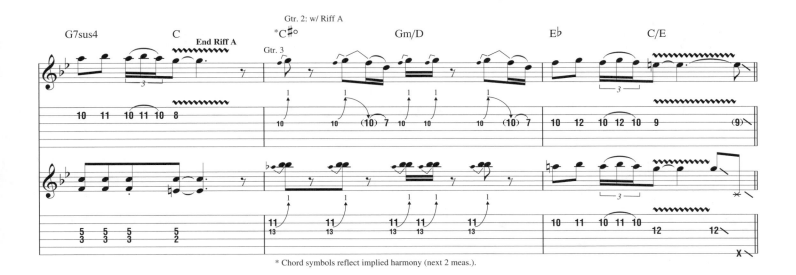

* Chord symbols reflect implied harmony (next 2 meas.).

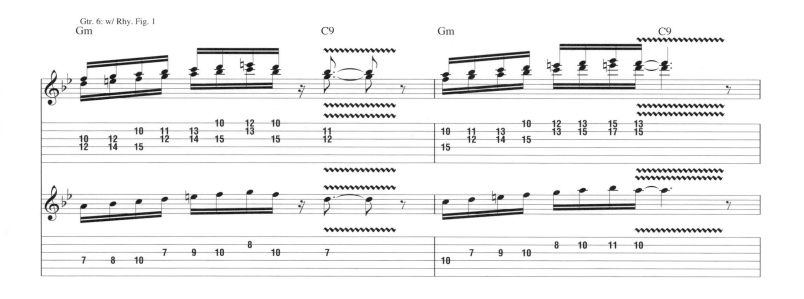

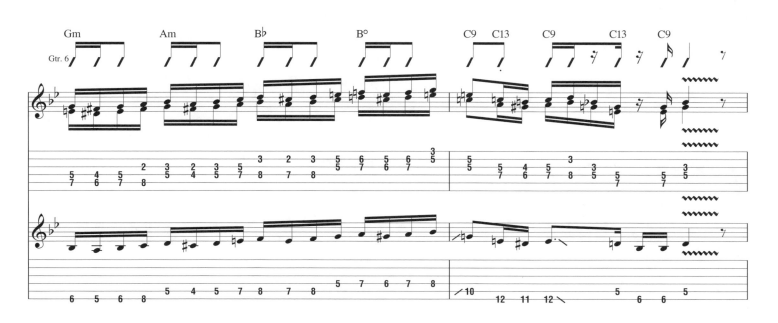

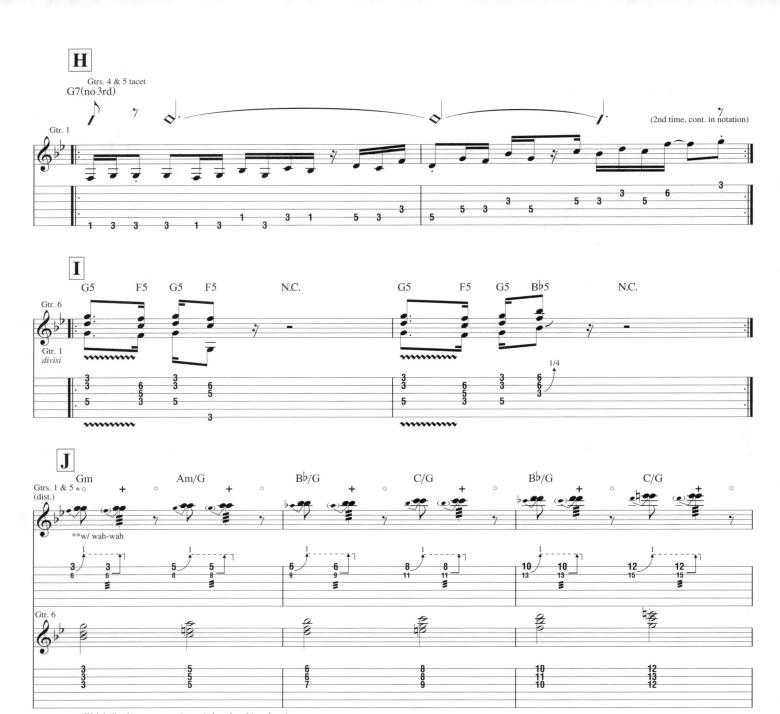

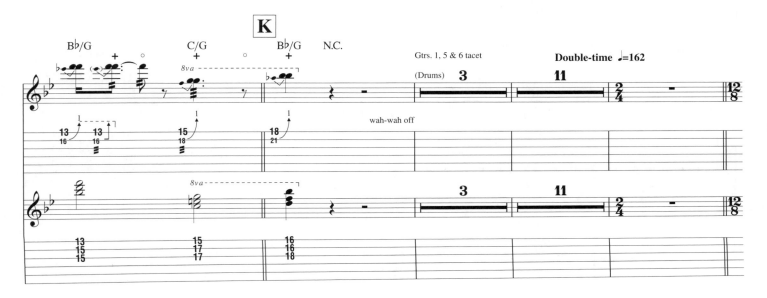

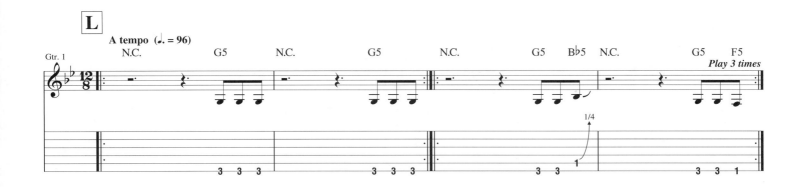

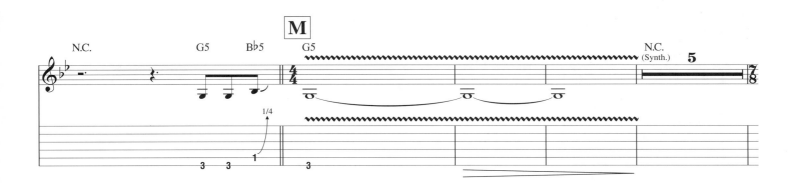

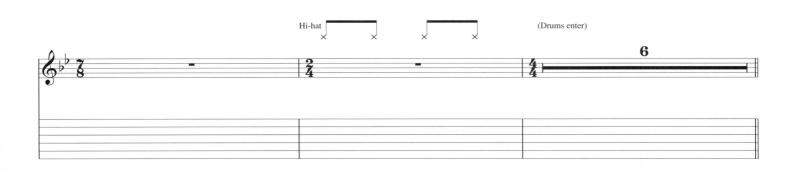

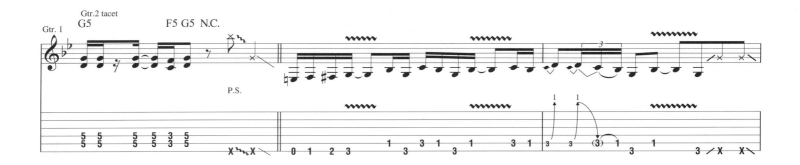

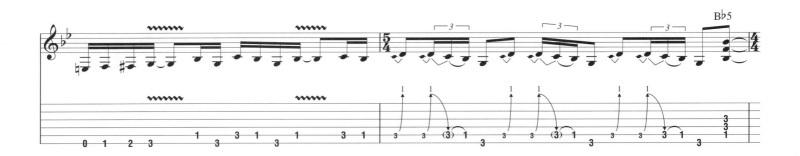

Free time

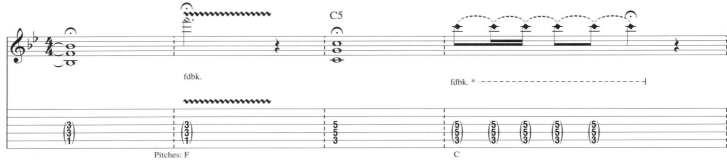

Pitches: F

C

* Using a guitar with Les Paul style electronics, set lead volume to 0 and rhythm volume to 10. Strike the strings while the pickup selector switch is in the lead position, then flip the switch in the rhythm indicated to simulate the re-attack.

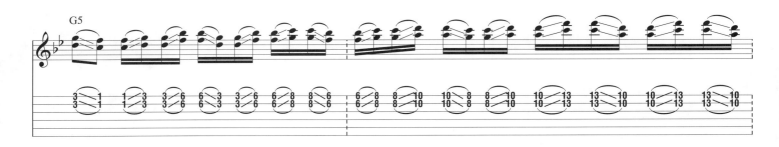

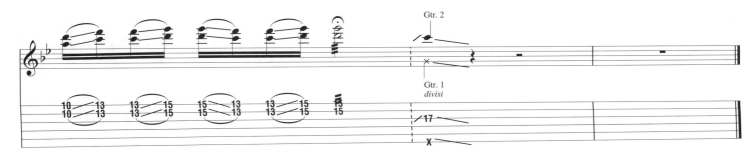

Free Bird

Words and Music by Allen Collins and Ronnie Van Zant

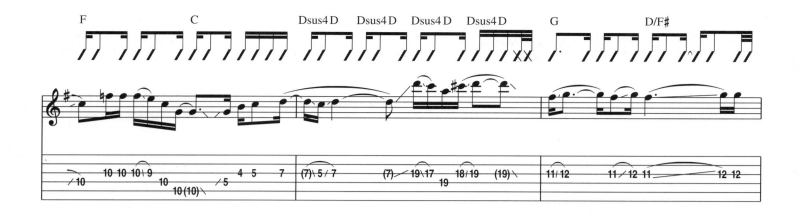

Verse

Gtr. 1: w/ Rhy. Fig. 1A, 2 times
Gtr. 2: w/ Rhy. Fig. 1, 4 times

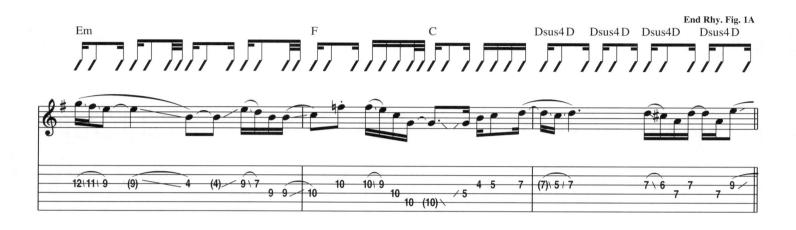

1. If I ___ leave ___ here to-mor - row, _____ would you _ still re-mem - ber me?_

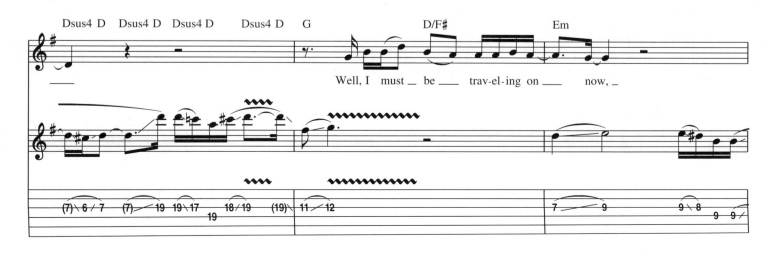

Well, I must _ be ___ trav-el-ing on ___ now, _

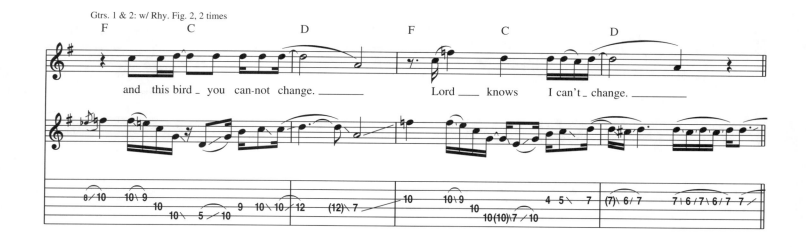

and this bird _ you can-not change. _____   Lord _____ knows   I can't _ change. _____

Interlude

Gtr. 1: w/ Rhy. Fig. 1A
Gtr. 2: w/ Rhy. Fig. 1, 2 times

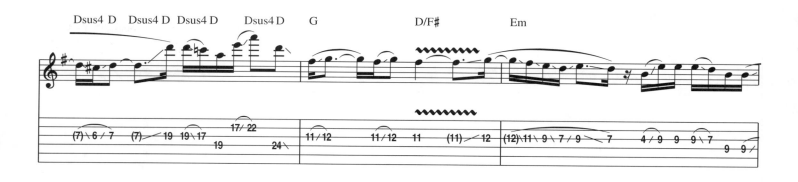

Verse

Gtr. 1: w/ Rhy. Fig. 1A, 2 times
Gtr. 2: w/ Rhy. Fig. 1, 4 times

2. Bye _ bye, ba - by, it's been   sweet_

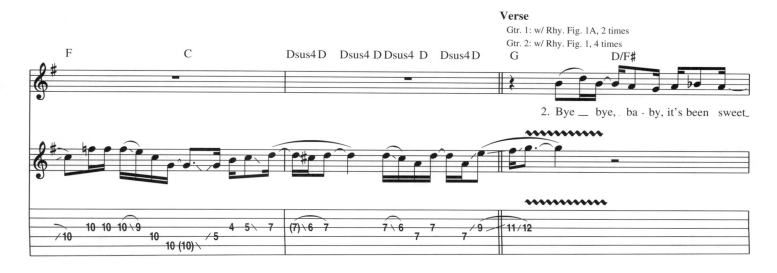

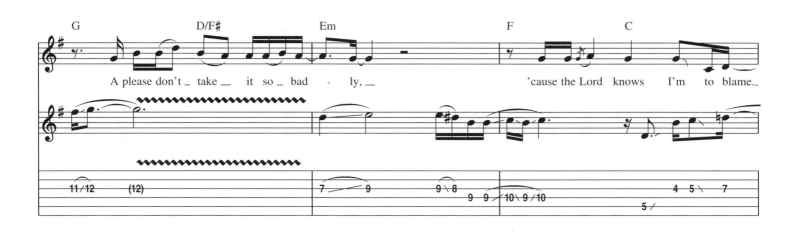

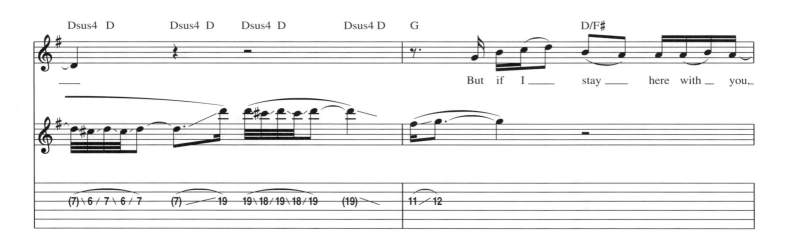

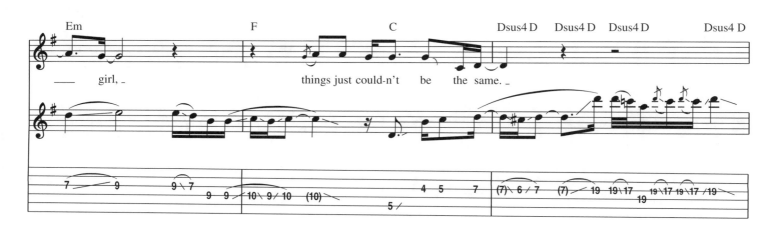

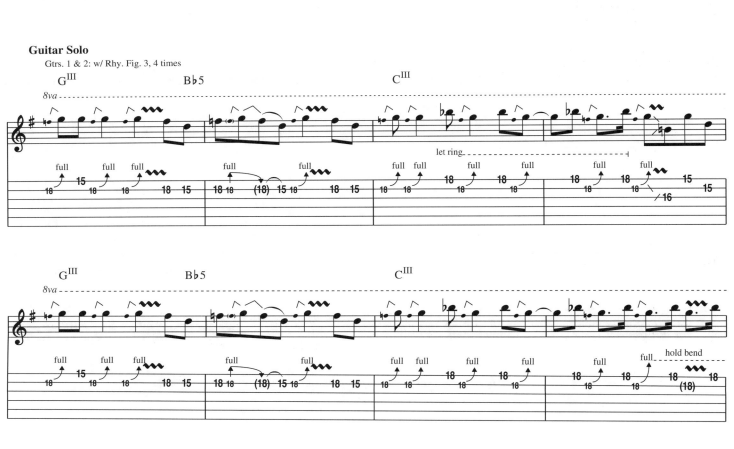

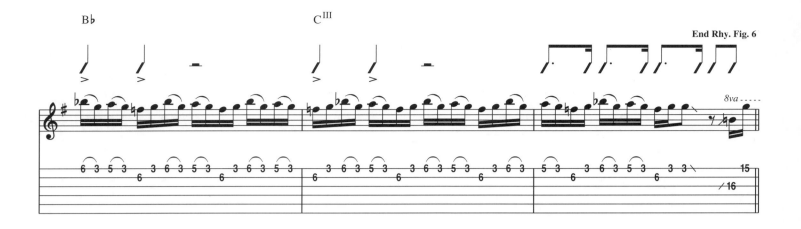

Gtrs. 1 & 2: w/ Rhy. Fig. 6, 3 times

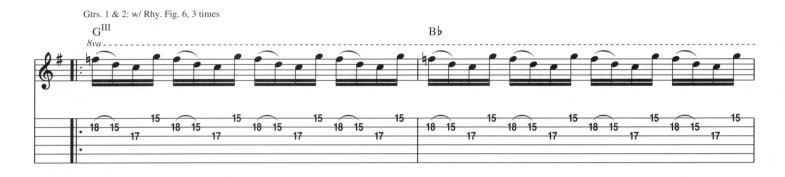

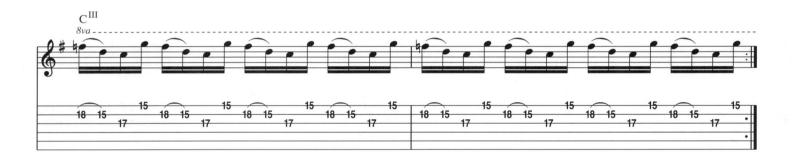

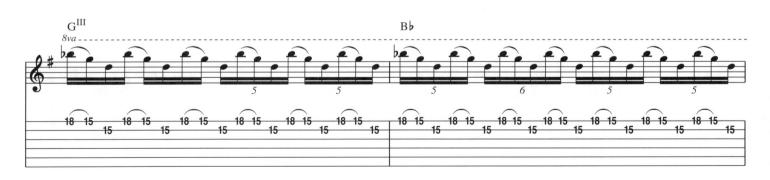

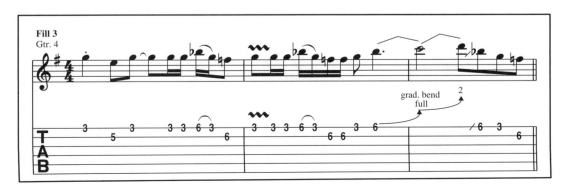

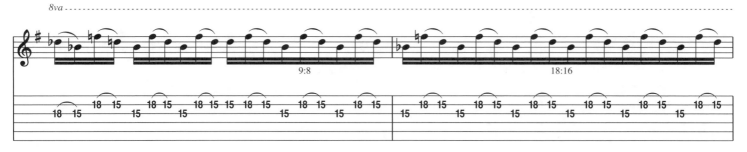

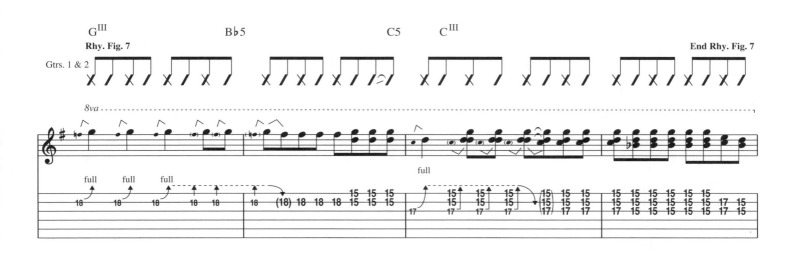

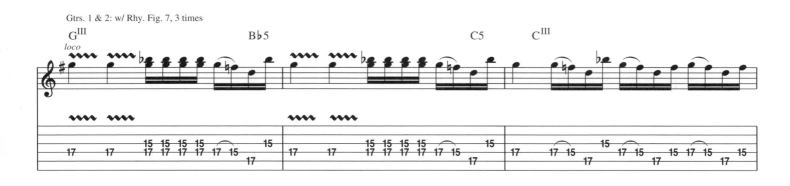

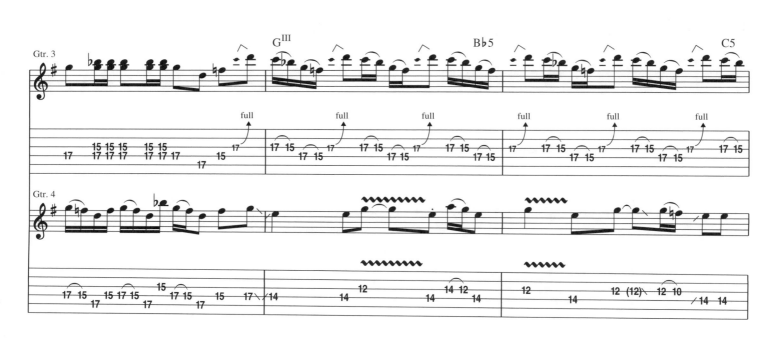

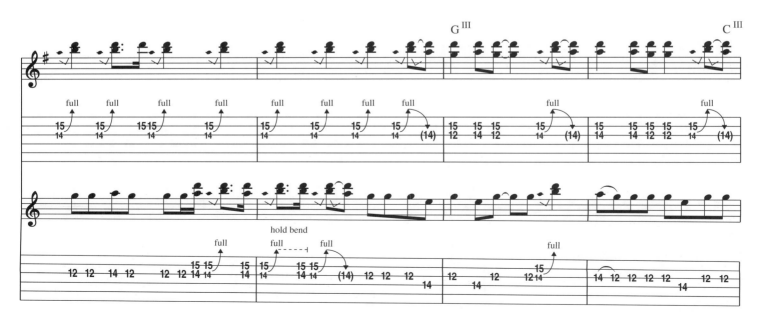

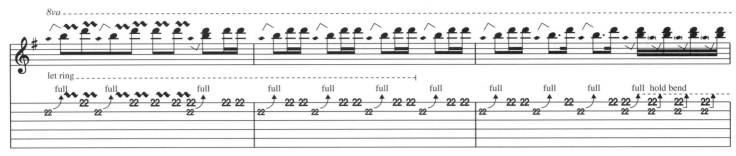

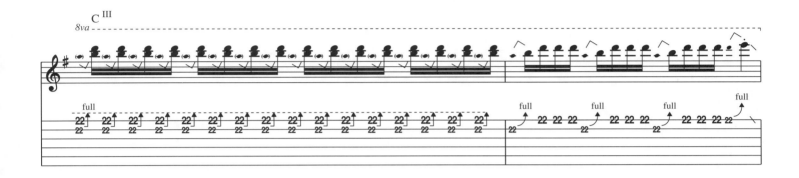

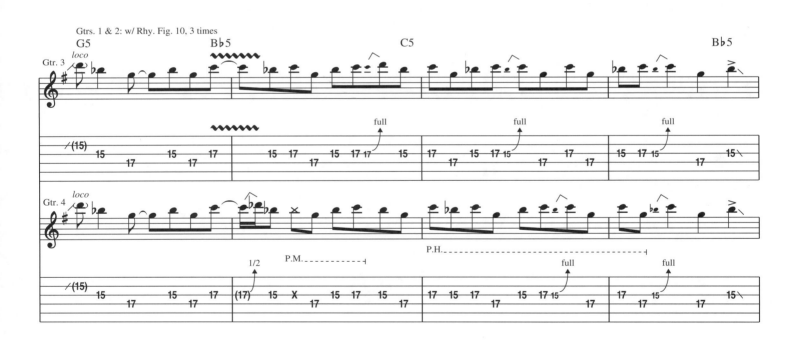

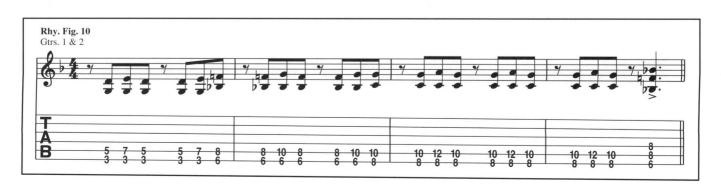

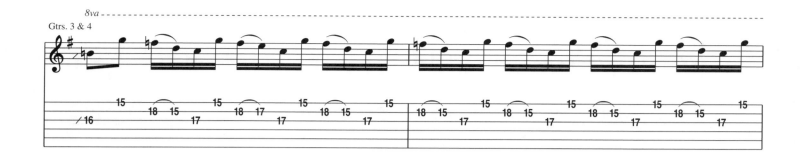

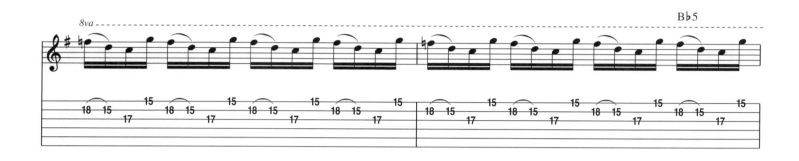

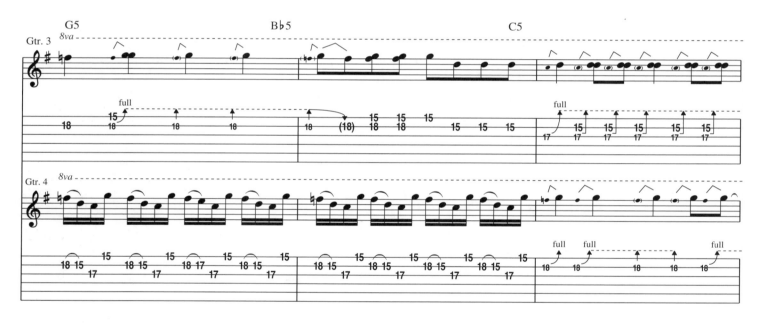

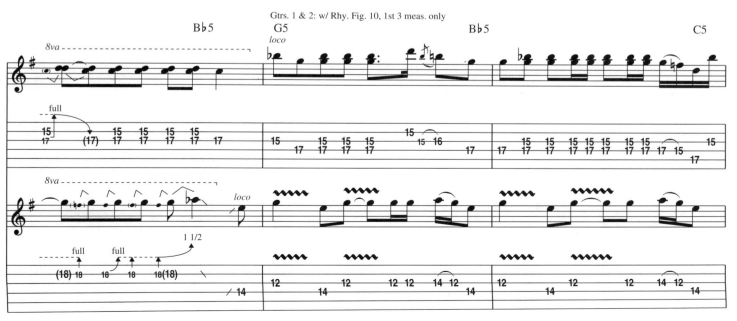

83

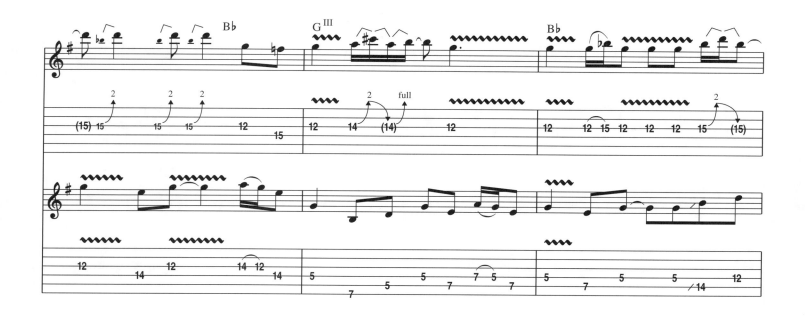

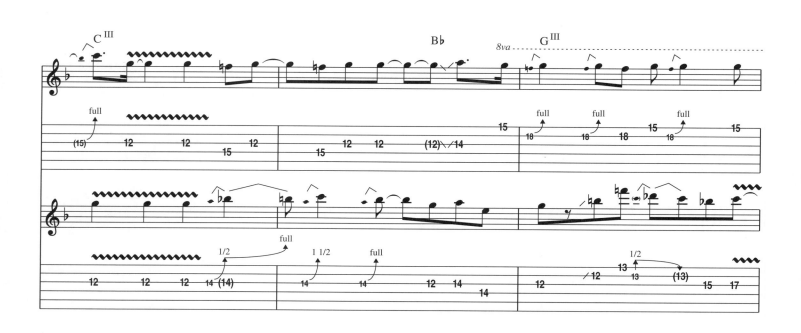

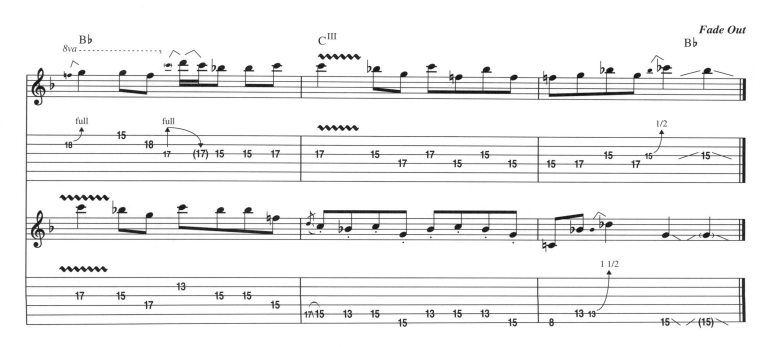

Godzilla

Words and Music by Donald Roeser

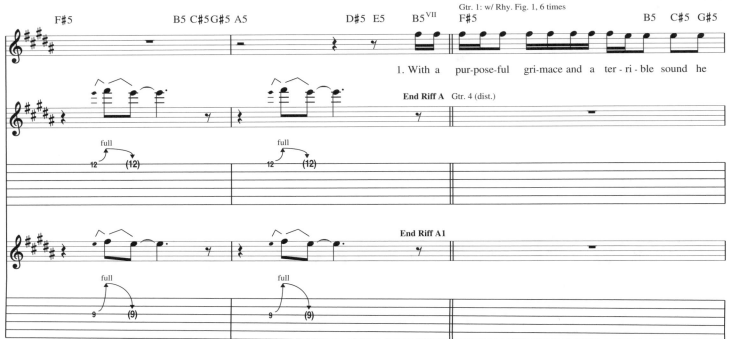

*Two gtrs. arr. for one.

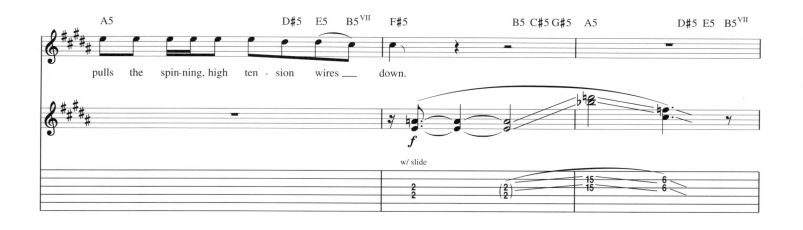

pulls the spin-ning, high ten - sion wires ___ down.

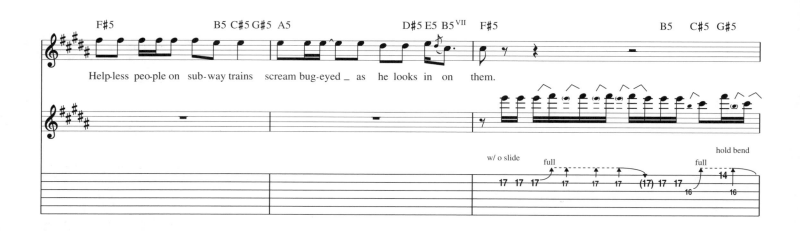

Help-less peo-ple on sub-way trains scream bug-eyed _ as he looks in on them.

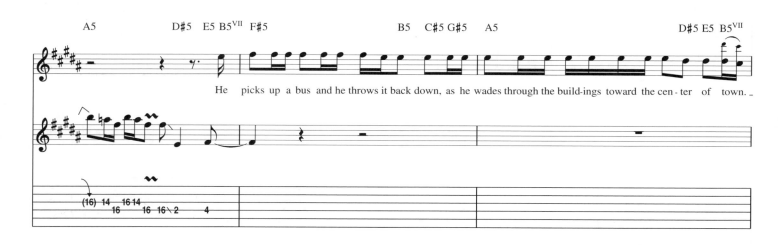

He picks up a bus and he throws it back down, as he wades through the build-ings toward the cen - ter of town. _

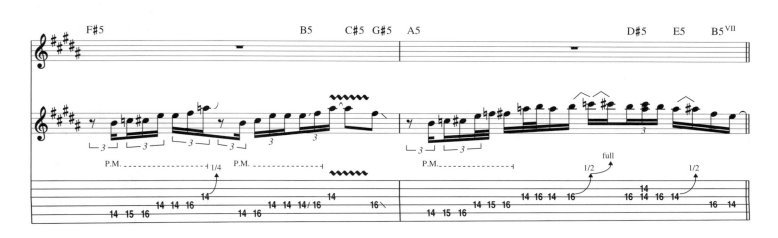

there goes To-kyo. Go, go God - zil-la. Whoo.

Outro

Gtr. 1: w/ Rhy. Fig. 1, 9 times, simile
Gtrs. 2 & 3: w/ Riffs A & A1

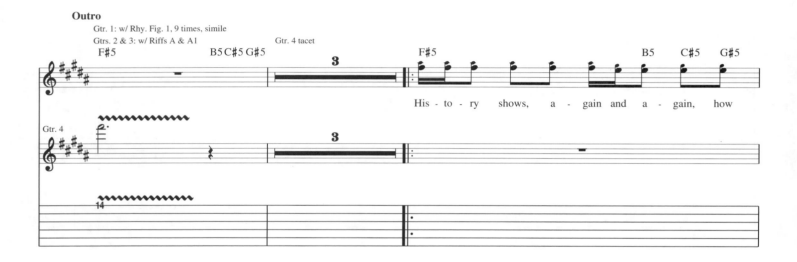

His - to - ry shows, a - gain and a - gain, how

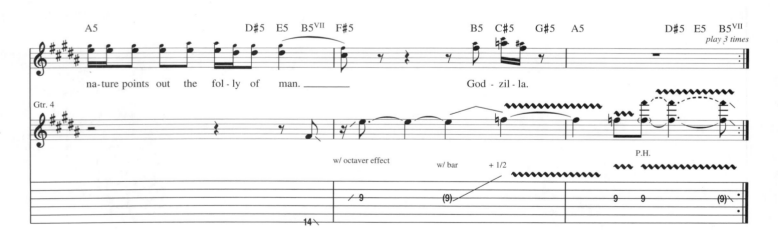

na-ture points out the fol - ly of man. God - zil - la.

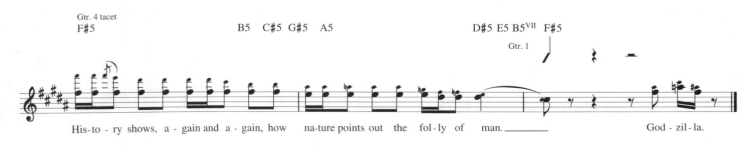

His - to - ry shows, a - gain and a - gain, how na-ture points out the fol - ly of man. God - zil - la.

Heart Shaped Box

Words and Music by Kurt Cobain

Drop D tuning, down 1/2 step:
(low to high) D♭-A♭-D♭-G♭-B♭-E♭

Intro

Moderately ♩ = 100

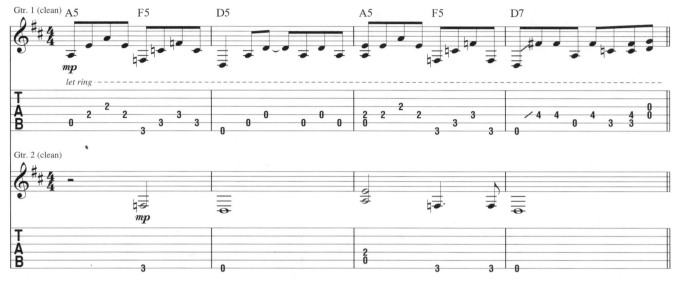

1., 3. She _ eyes me like _ a Pi - sces when _ I am weak. _

Fill 2
Gtr. 2

Fill 3
Gtr. 2

I wish I could eat ___ your can - cer when ___ you ___ turn black. _

Chorus

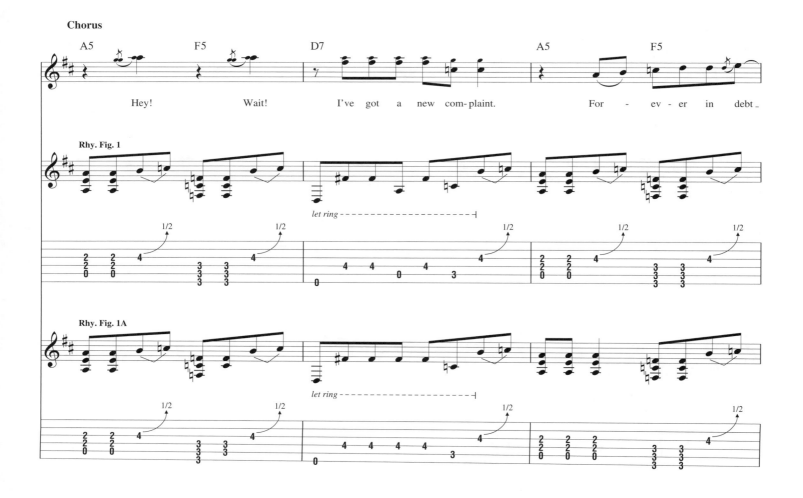

Hey! Wait! I've got a new com - plaint. For - ev - er in debt _

Rhy. Fig. 1

Rhy. Fig. 1A

to your price - less ad - vice. ___ Hey! Wait! I've got a new com-plaint.

For - ev - er in debt ___ to your price - less ad - vice. ___ Hey! Wait!

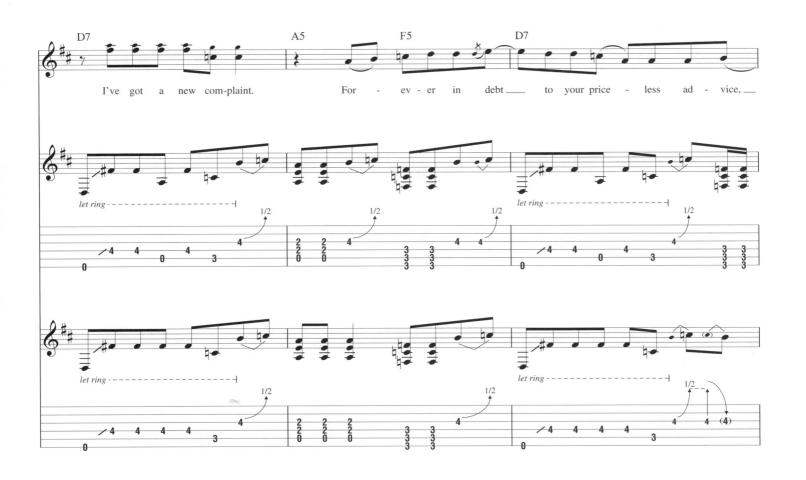

I've got a new com-plaint. For - ev - er in debt ____ to your price - less ad - vice, ____

To Coda ⊕

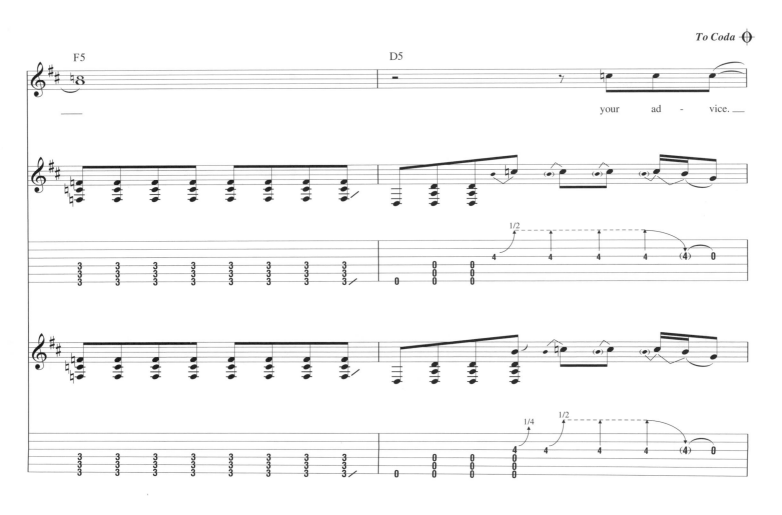

your ad - vice. ____

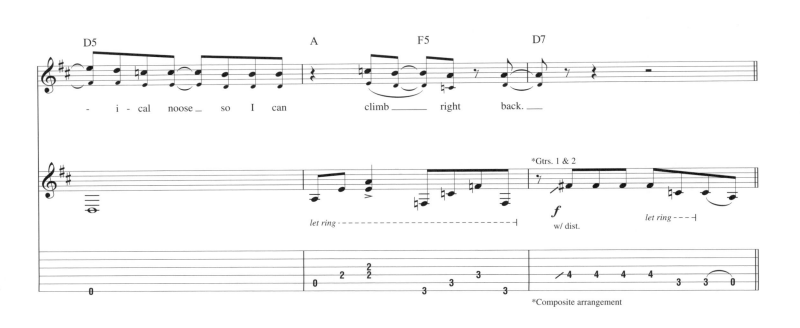

Chorus
Gtrs. 1 & 2: w/ Rhy. Figs. 1 & 1A

Hey! Wait! I've got a new com-plaint. For - ev - er in debt ___

___ to your price - less ad - vice. ___ Hey! Wait! I've got a new com-plaint.

For - ev - er in debt ___ to your price - less ad - vice. ___ Hey! Wait!

I've got a new com-plaint. For - ev - er in debt ___ to your price - less ad - vice, ___

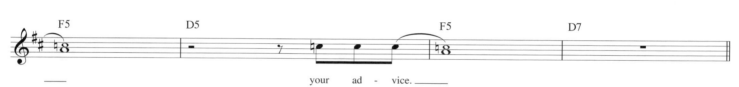

___ your ad - vice. ___

Guitar Solo

Gtr. 1

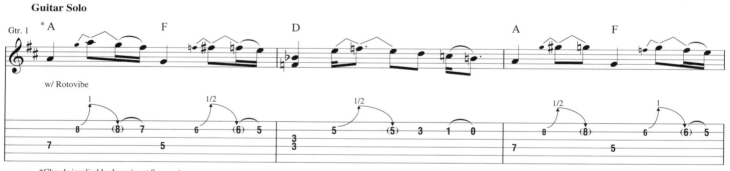

w/ Rotovibe

*Chords implied by bass (next 8 meas.)

D.S. al Coda

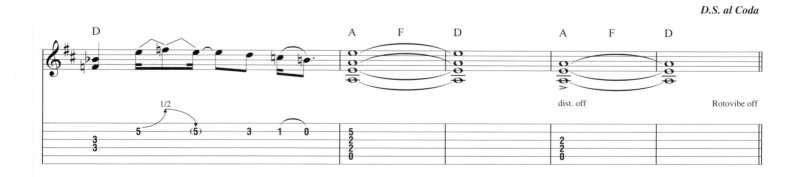

dist. off   Rotovibe off

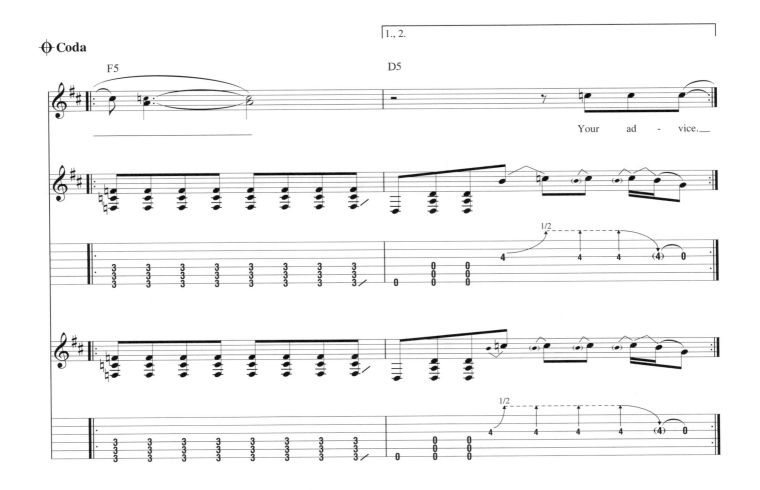

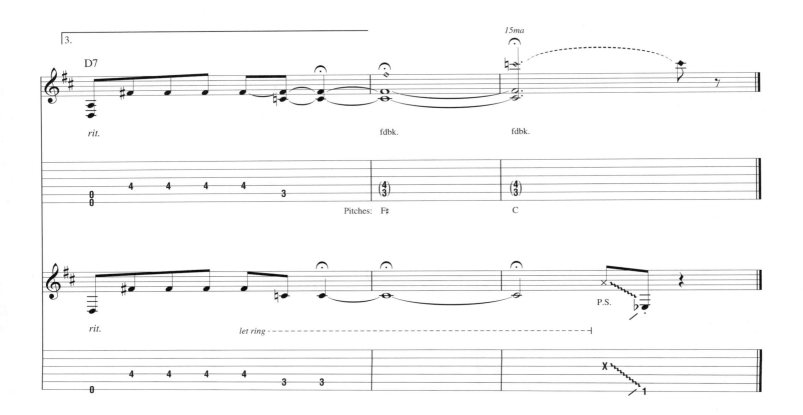

Higher Ground

Words and Music by Stevie Wonder

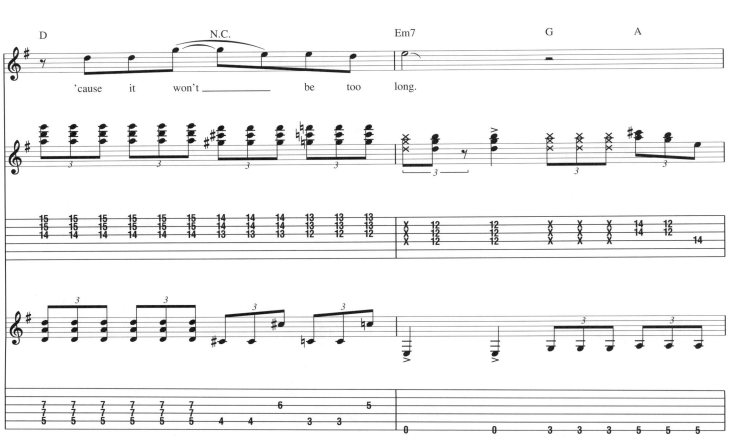

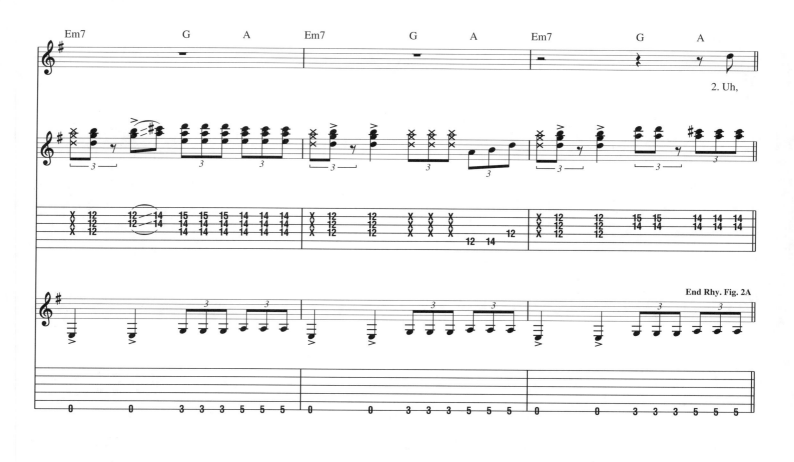

2. Uh,

End Rhy. Fig. 2A

Verse

Gtr. 2: w/ Rhy. Fig. 1 (2 times)
Gtr. 1: w/ Rhy. Fill 1 (4 times)

E5 | G5 A5 E5 | G5 A5 E5 | G5 A5 E5 | G5 A5

pow - ers _____ a keep on ly - in', _____ while your

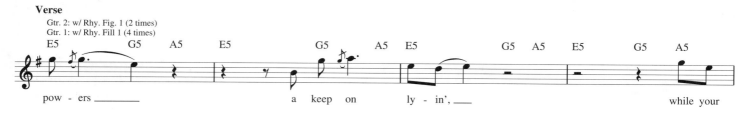

E5 | G5 A5 E5 | G5 A5 E5 | G5 A5 E5 | G5 A5

peo - ple _____ a keep on dy - in'. _____ Uh,

Gtrs. 1 & 2: w/ Rhy. Figs. 2 & 2A   Gtr. 1: w/ Rhy. Fill 2

F#m7 | A B F#m7 | A B A | D | N.C.

world, keep on turn - in', _____ 'cause it won't _ a be too

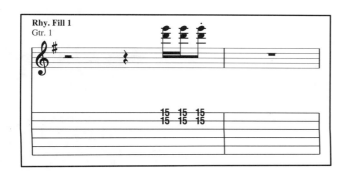

Rhy. Fill 1
Gtr. 1

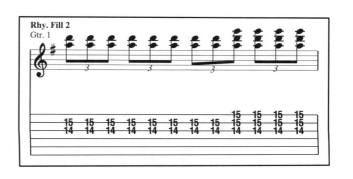

Rhy. Fill 2
Gtr. 1

104

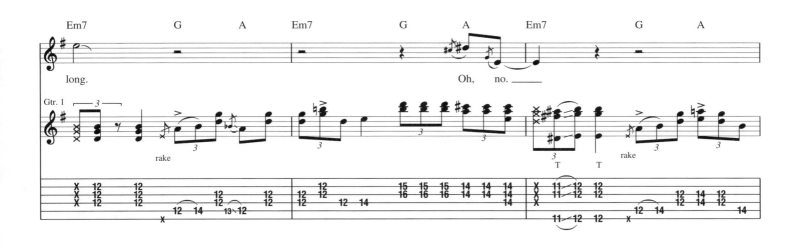

To Coda
Em7 F#5 B7#5
than I knew then. Gon - na keep on try - in' till I reach the high - est
P.M. P.M.
* T
let ring
w/ bar
* T = Thumb on 6th str.
Em7 G A Em7 G A Em7 G A Em7 G A
ground. 3. Uh,
rake
1/2 1/2
Riff A
End Riff A
Verse
Gtr. 2: w/ Rhy. Fig. 1 (2 times)
E5 G5 A5 E5 G5 A5 E5 G5 A5 E5 G5 A5
teach - ers, a keep on teach - in'. Uh,

Verse

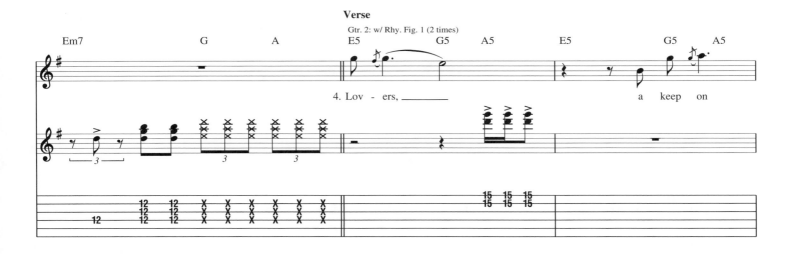

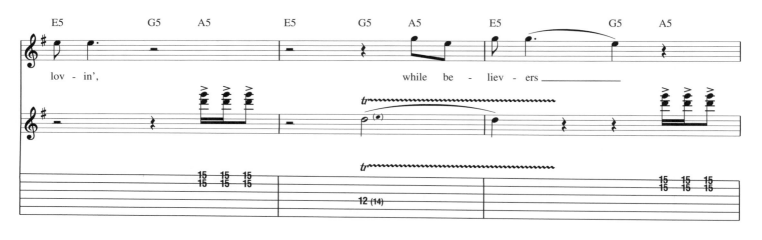

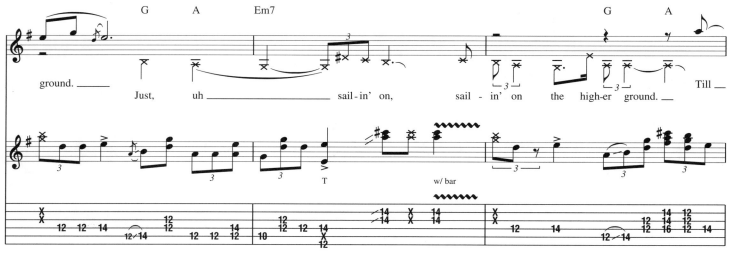

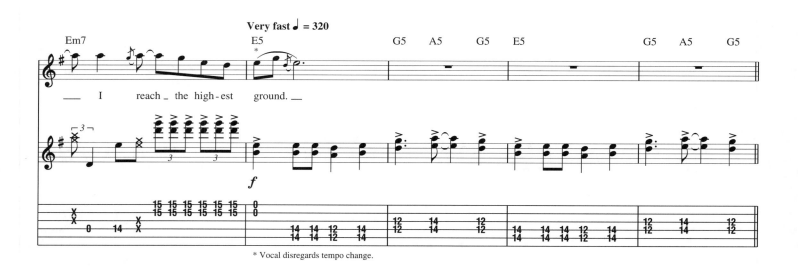

* Vocal disregards tempo change.

** Composite arrangement.

I Love Rock 'N Roll

Words and Music by Alan Merrill and Jake Hooker

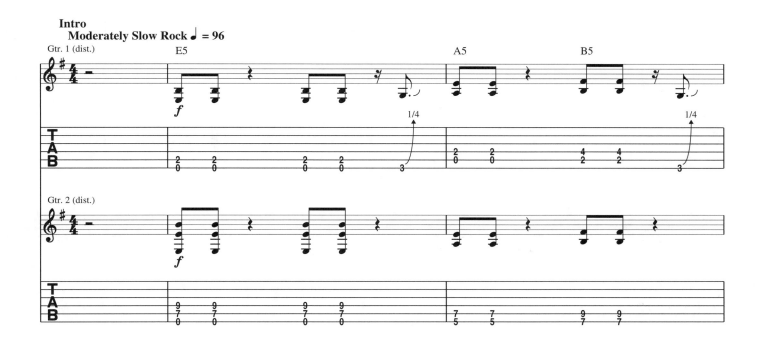

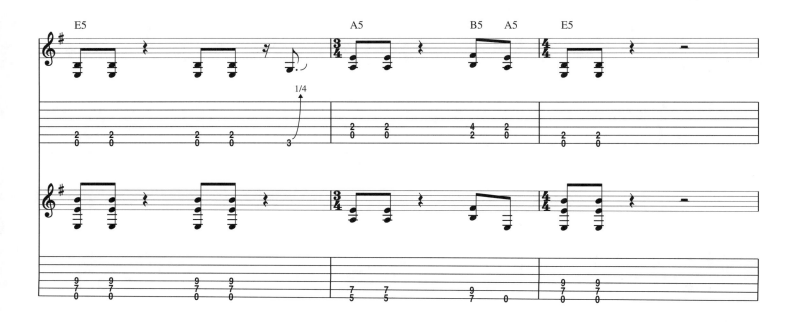

Verse

1. I saw him danc-in' there, __ by the re-cord ma-chine.
smiled, so I got up __ and asked for his name. I

simile on repeat

knew he must have been __ a-bout sev-en-teen.
"That don't mat-ter," he said, "'cause it's all the same." The beat was go-in' strong, __
I said, "Can I take ya home __ where

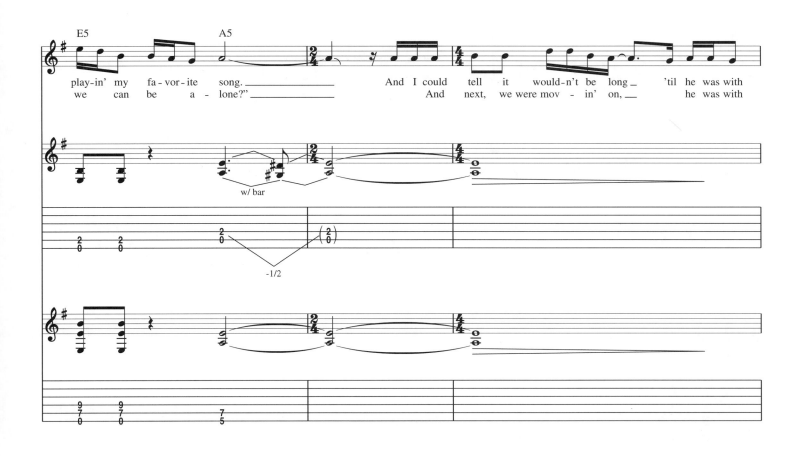

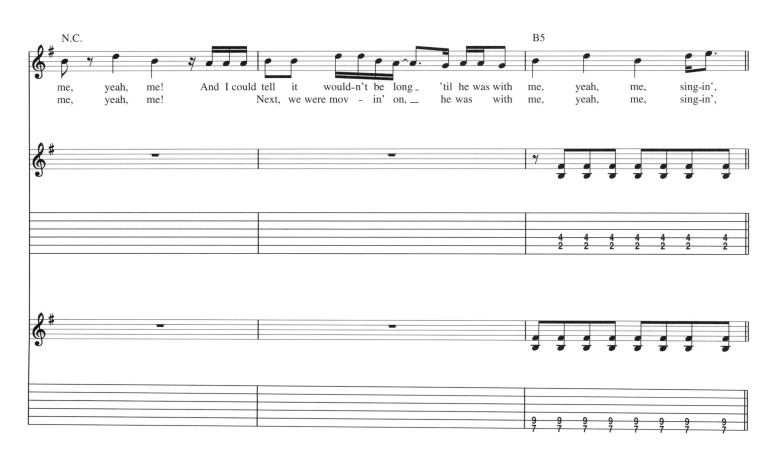

Chorus

I love rock 'n' roll, _ so put an-oth-er dime in the juke box, - ba - by. I love rock 'n' roll, _ so

come and take your time and dance with me. Ow! 2. He

Guitar Solo/Pre-Chorus

Said, "Can I take ya home where we can be a-

lone?" _____ Next, we were mov - in' on, __ he was with me, yeah, me! And we'll be

Gtrs. 1 & 3 tacet

A5

w/ bar

-1/2

Gtr. 2 tacet
N.C.

Chorus
N.C.

mov - in' on, __ and sing - in' that same old song, yeah, with me, __ sing - in', I love rock 'n' roll, __ so

put an - oth - er dime in the juke - box, ba - by. I love rock 'n' roll, _ so come and take your time and dance with me.

Outro-Chorus

I love rock 'n' roll, _ so put an-oth-er dime in the juke-box, ba - by.

Gtr. 1

Gtr. 2

*Gtr. 3

*Play 3rd & 4th times only.

I love rock 'n' roll, _ so come and take your time and dance with   come and take your time and dance with me!

115

Iron Man

Words and Music by Frank Iommi, John Osbourne, William Ward and Terence Butler

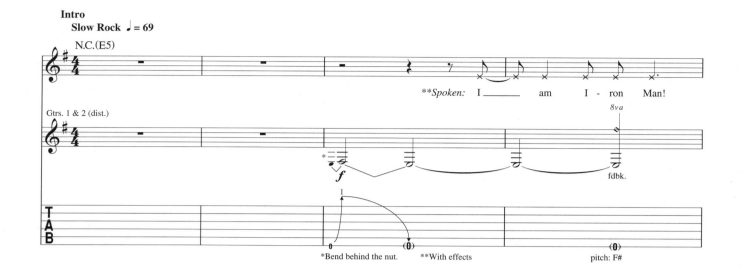

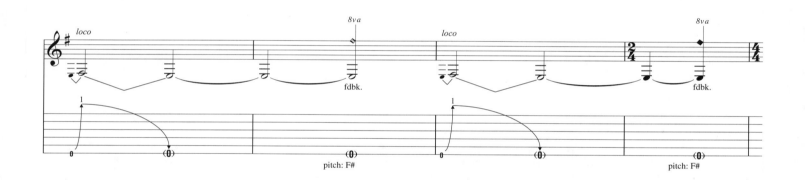

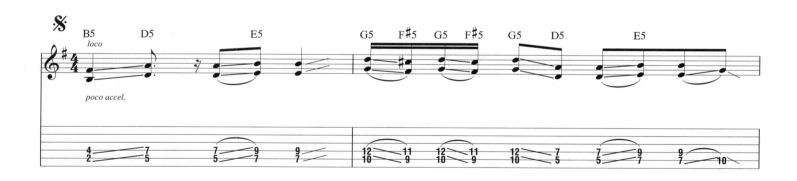

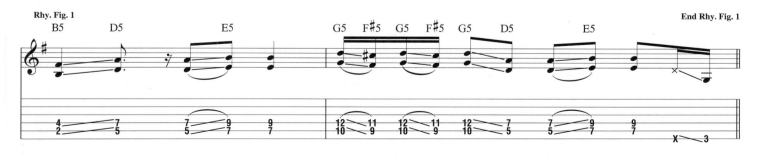

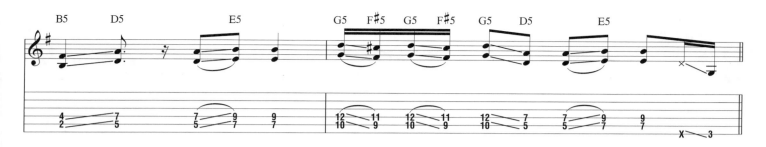

Verse

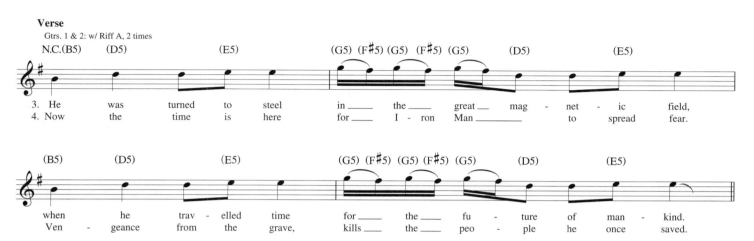

Gtrs. 1 & 2: w/ Riff A, 2 times

3. He was turned to steel in ___ the ___ great ___ mag - net - ic field,
4. Now the time is here for ___ I - ron Man ___ to spread fear.

when he trav - elled time for ___ the ___ fu - ture of man - kind.
Ven - geance from the grave, kills ___ the ___ peo - ple he once saved.

Bridge

No-bod - y wants ___ him, ___ he just stares ___ at the world. ___
No-bod - y wants ___ him, ___ they just turn ___ their ___ heads. ___

Gtrs. 1 & 2

Rhy. Fig. 2   End Rhy. Fig. 2   Riff B   End Riff B

Gtrs. 1 & 2: w/ Rhy. Fig. 2   Gtrs. 1 & 2: w/ Riff B

Plan - ning his ven - geance ___ that he will ___ soon un - furl. ___
No - bod - y helps ___ him, ___ now he has ___ his re - venge. ___

Interlude

Double - Time ♩ = 164

N.C. (C#m)

Gtrs. 1 & 2   Riff C   End Riff C

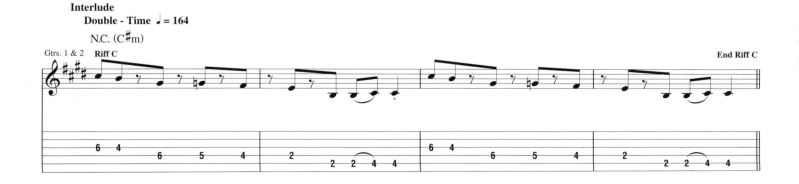

Guitar Solo
Gtr. 2 tacet

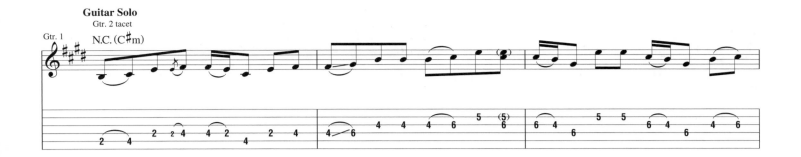

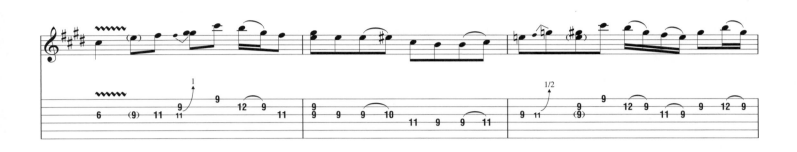

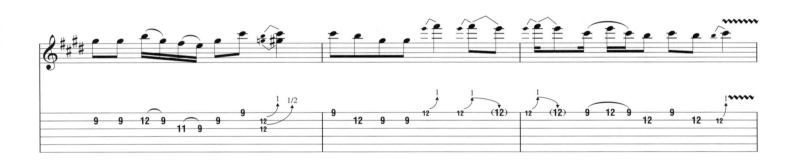

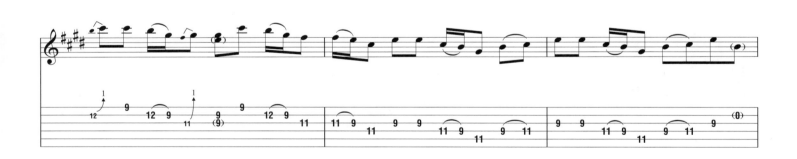

Interlude

D.S. al Coda
(take 2nd ending)

Gtrs. 1 & 2: w/ Riff B, 2 times

Coda

Double - Time ♩= 164

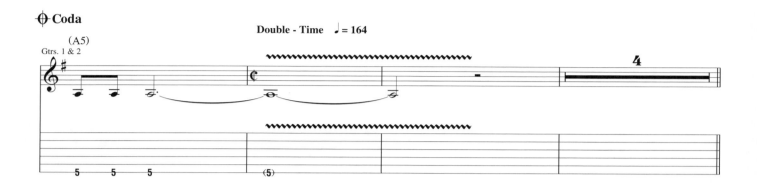

* Bend behind the nut.

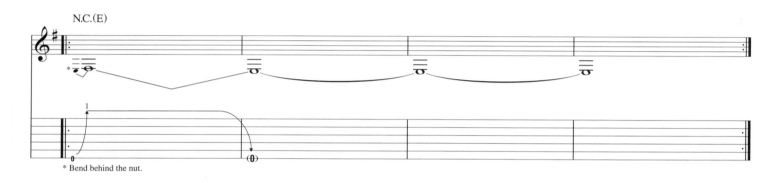

** Chords implied by bass.

Guitar Solo

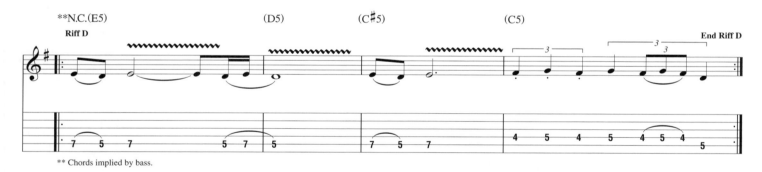

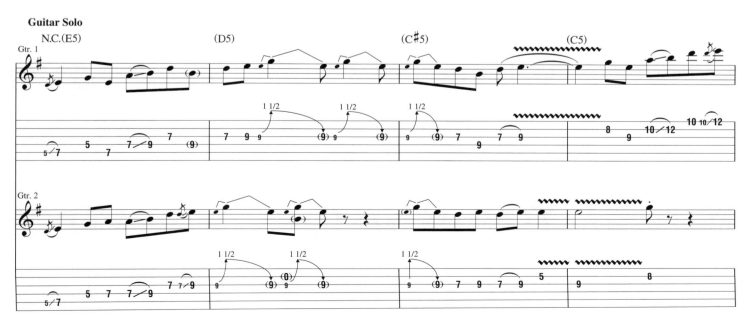

120

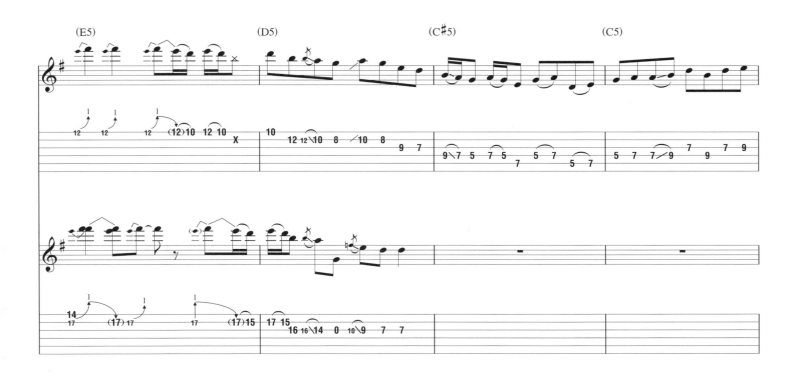

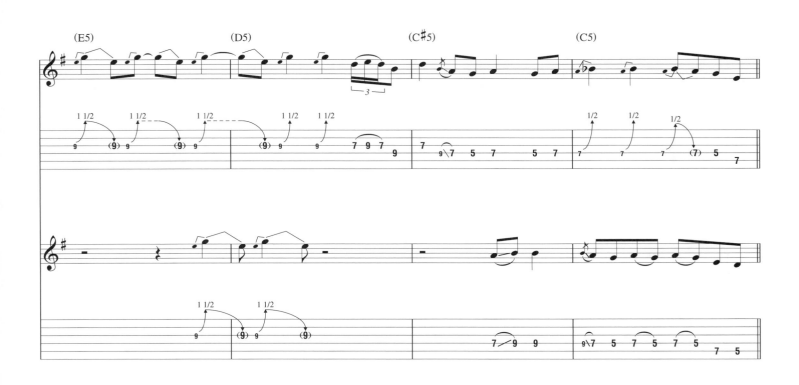

Outro

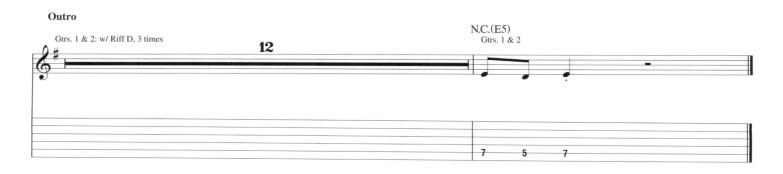

Jessica

Written by Dickey Betts

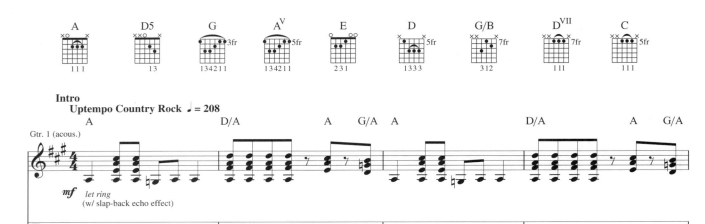

Intro

Uptempo Country Rock ♩ = 208

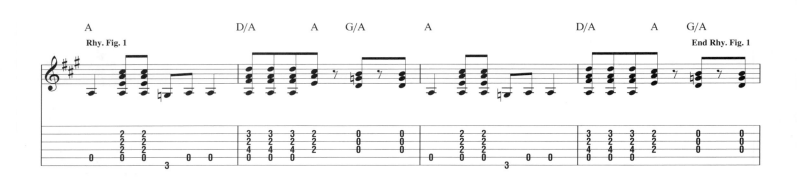

Chorus

Gtr. 1: w/ Rhy. Fig. 1, 3 times

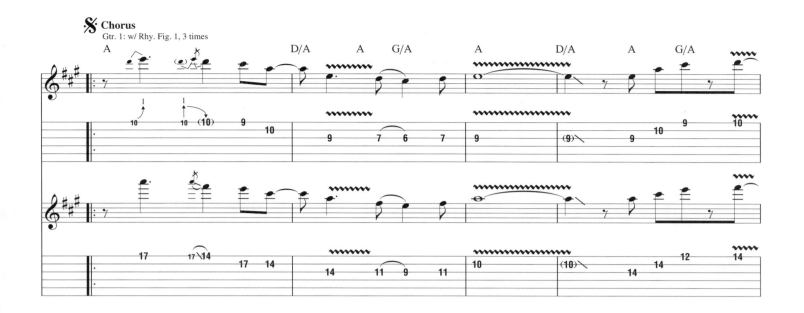

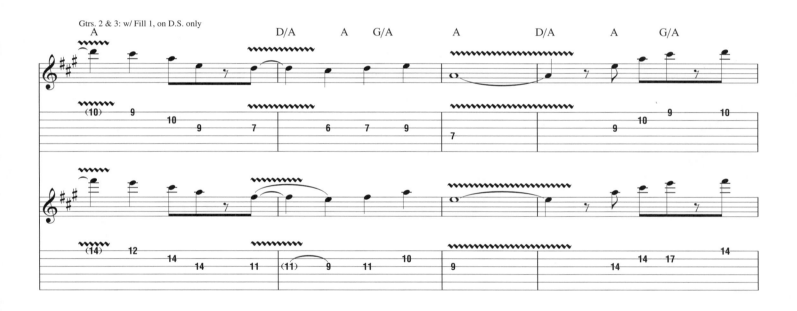

Gtrs. 2 & 3: w/ Fill 1, on D.S. only

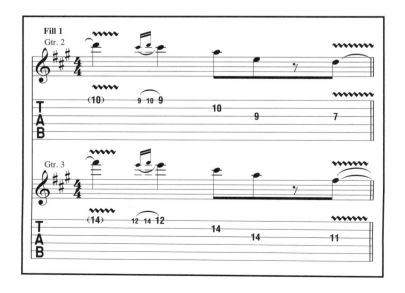

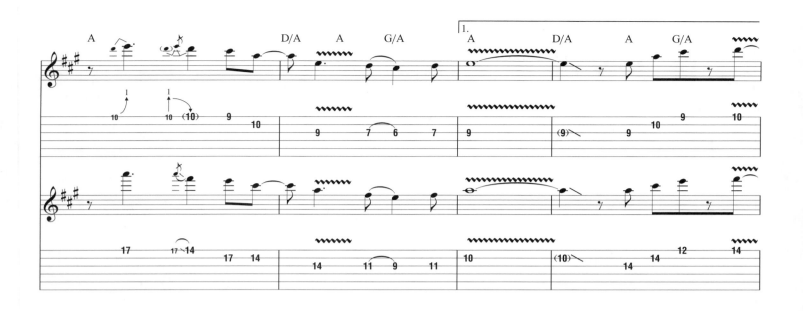

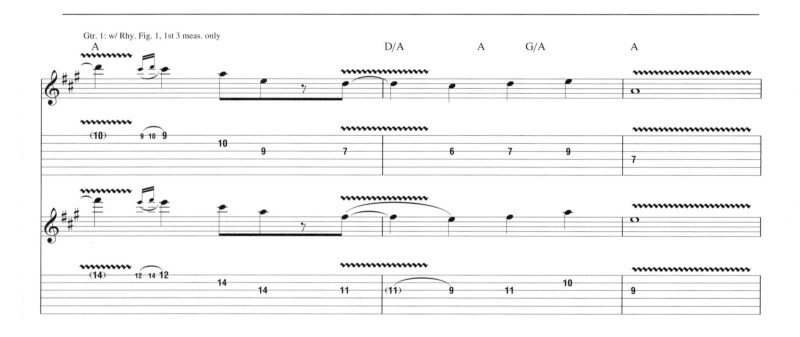

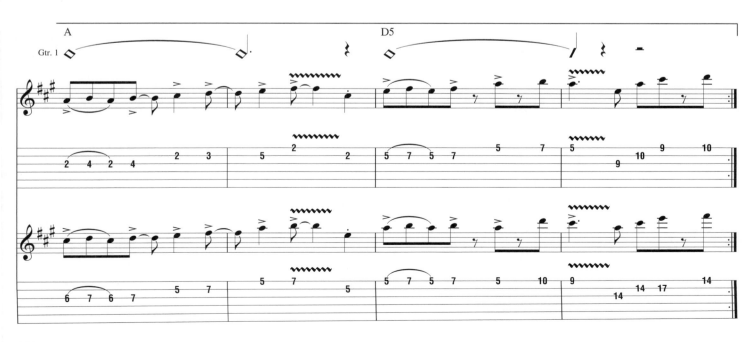

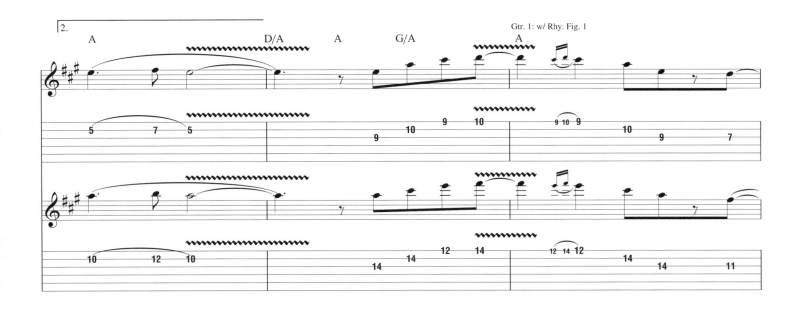

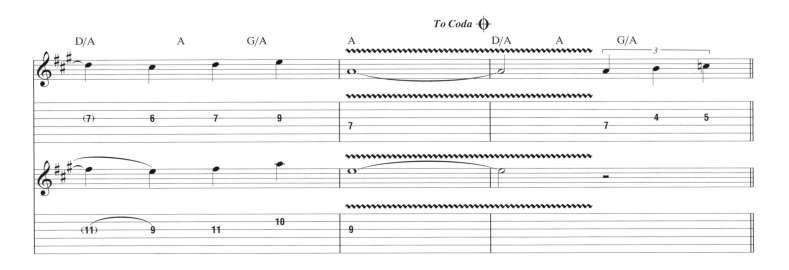

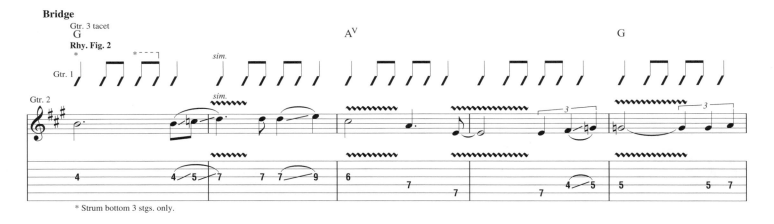

* Strum bottom 3 stgs. only.

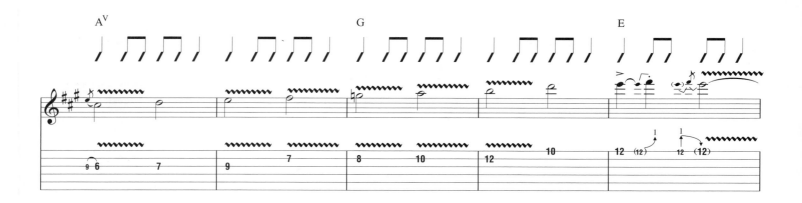

Chorus

Gtr. 1: w/ Rhy. Fig. 1, 3 times

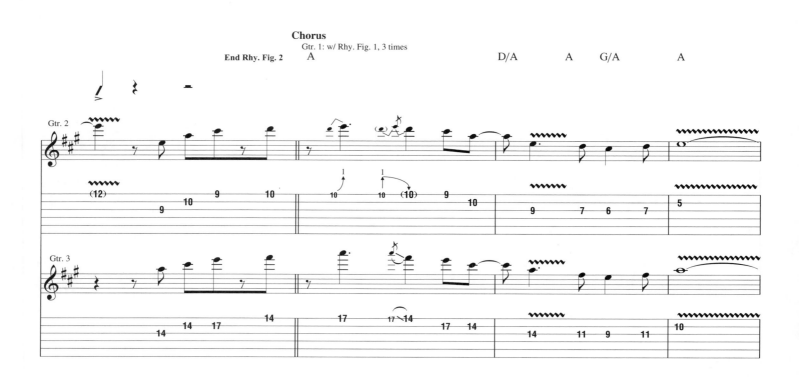

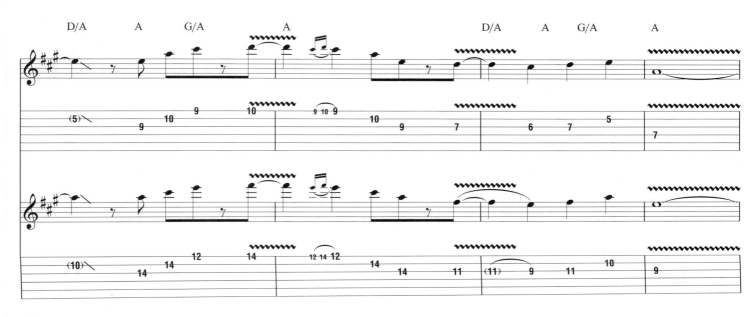

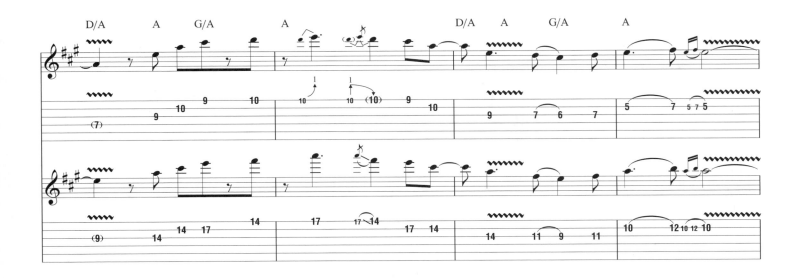

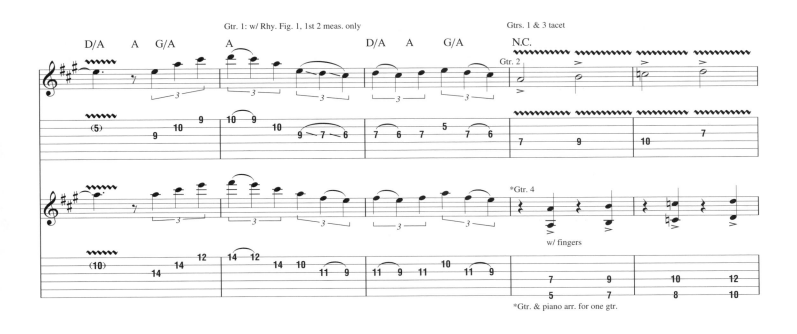

Gtr. 1: w/ Rhy. Fig. 1, 1st 2 meas. only

Gtrs. 1 & 3 tacet

*Gtr. & piano arr. for one gtr.

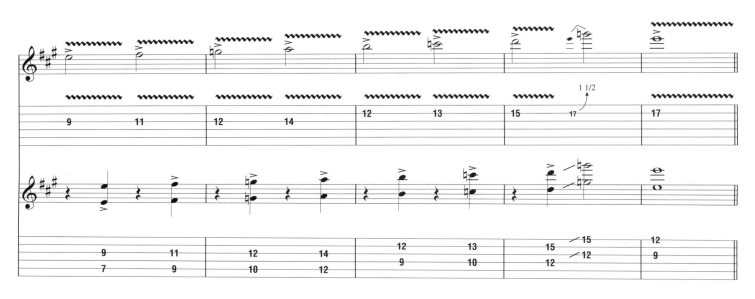

Breakdown

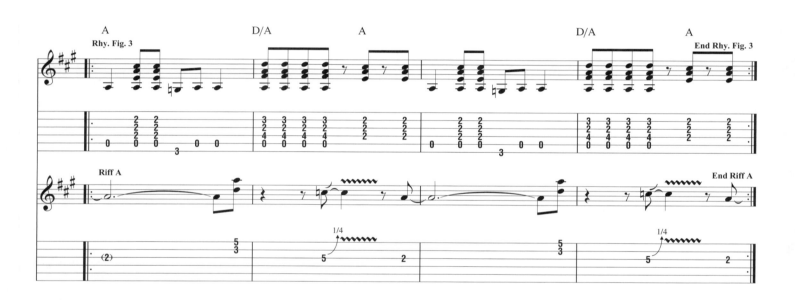

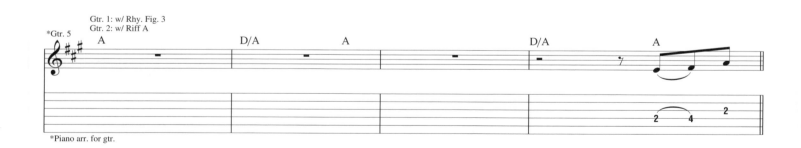

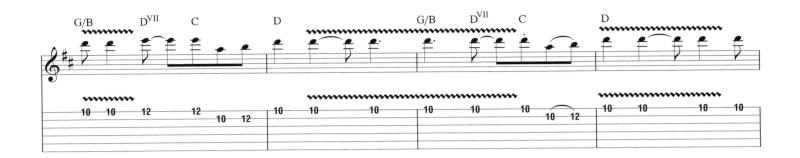

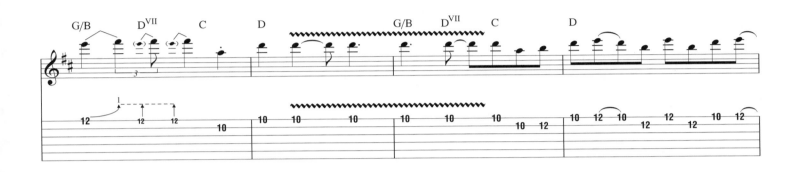

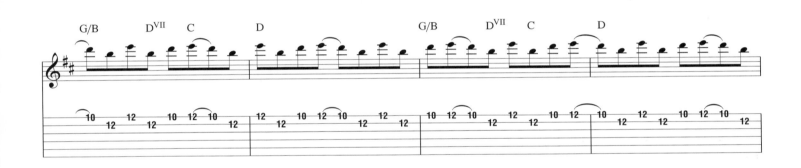

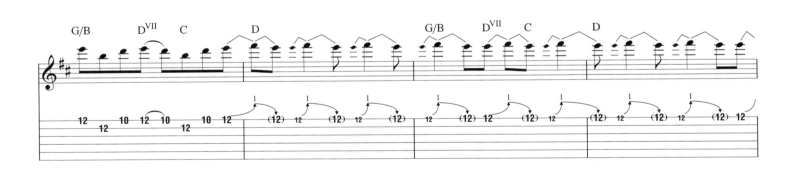

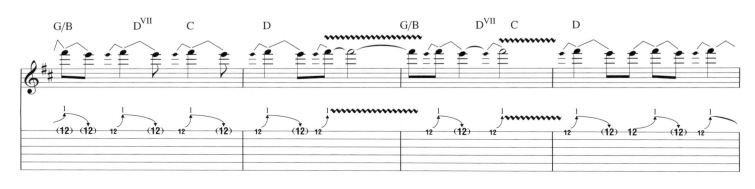

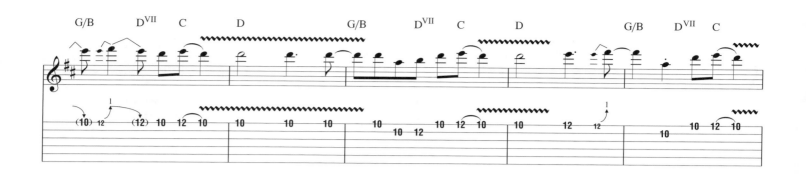

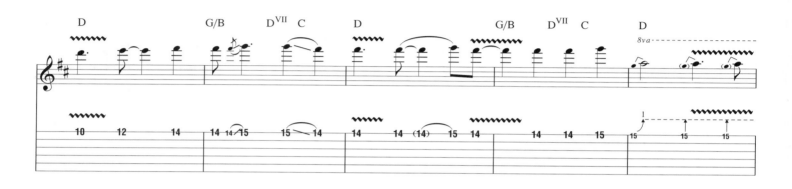

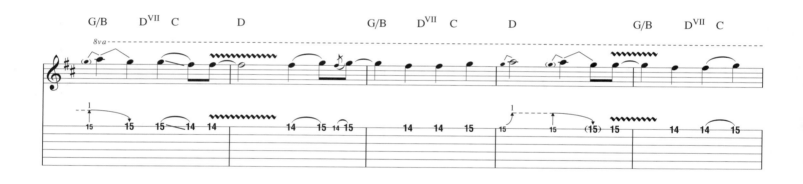

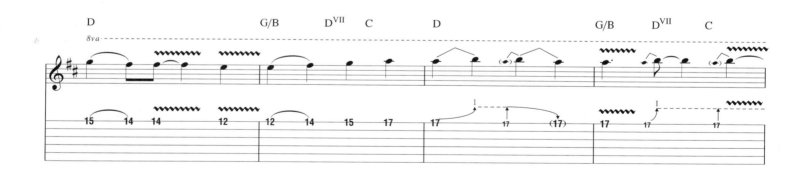

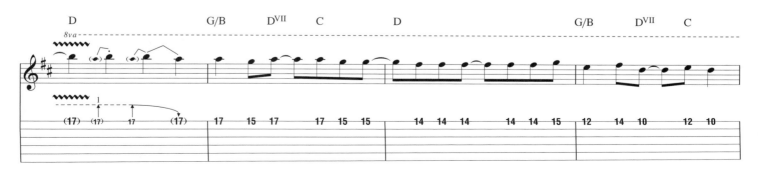

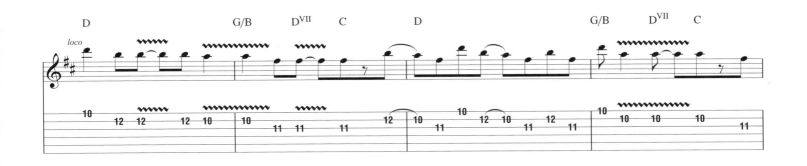

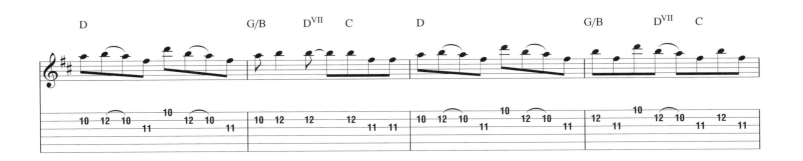

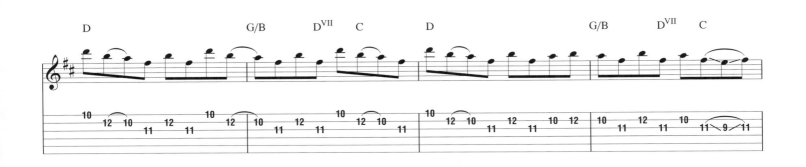

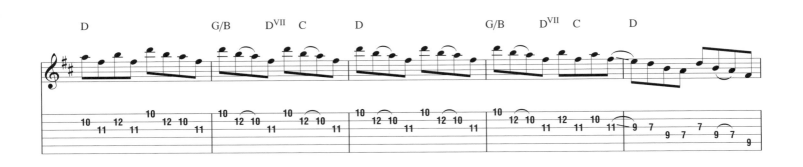

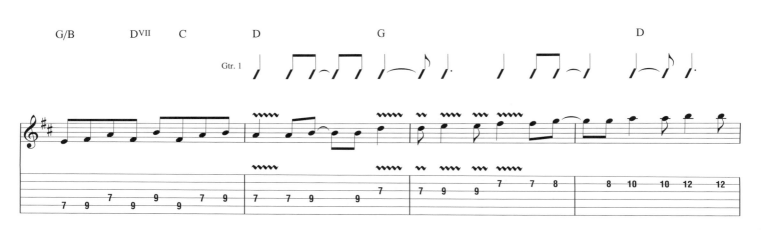

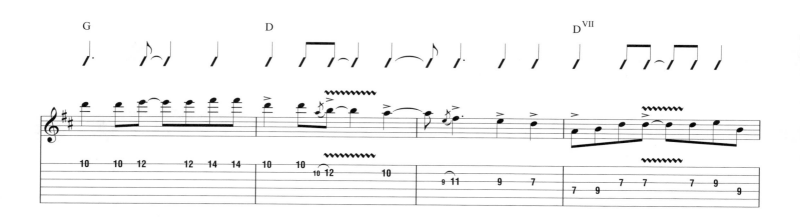

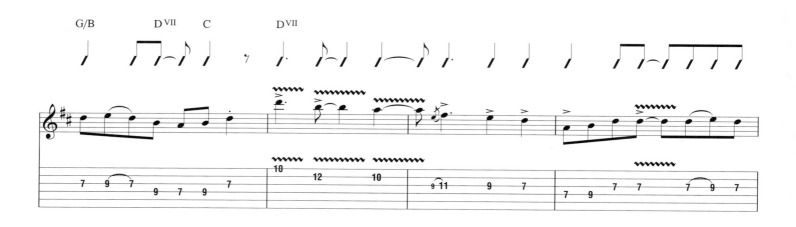

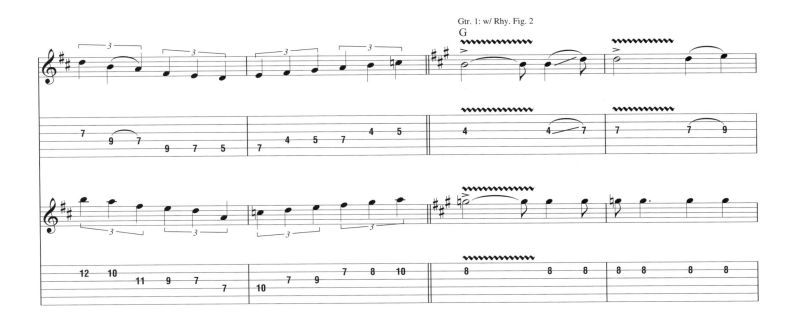

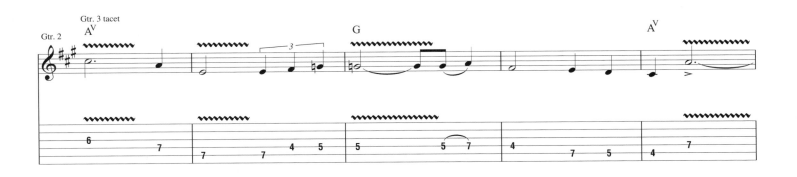

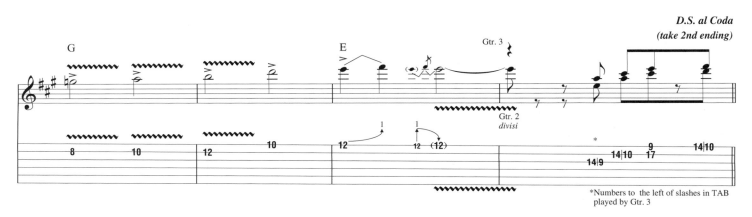

*Numbers to the left of slashes in TAB
played by Gtr. 3

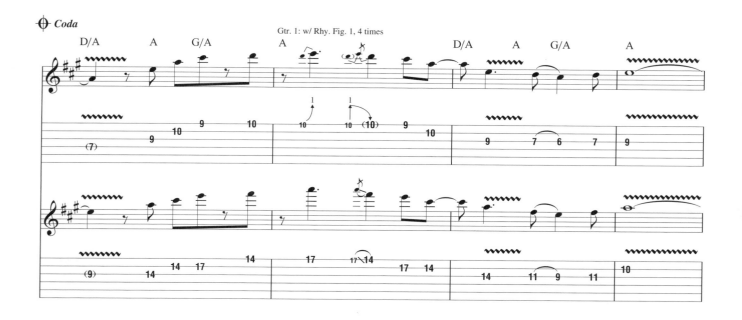

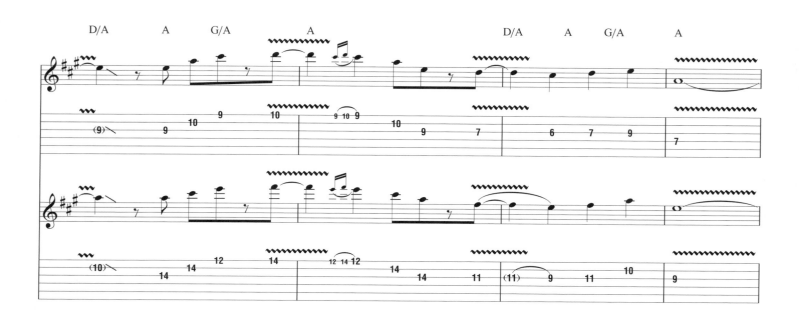

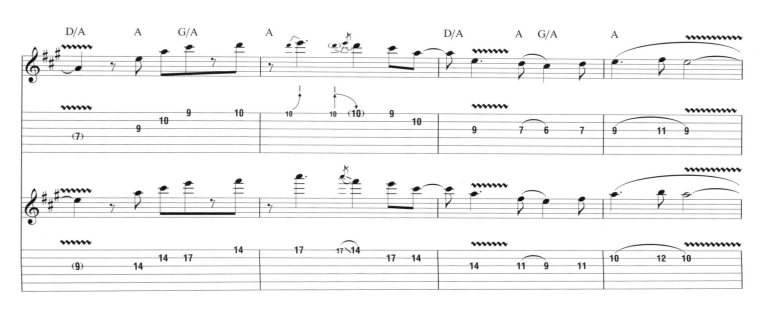

Killer Queen

Words and Music by Freddie Mercury

Verse

2. To a - void com - pli - ca - tions, she nev - er kept the same ad - dress.

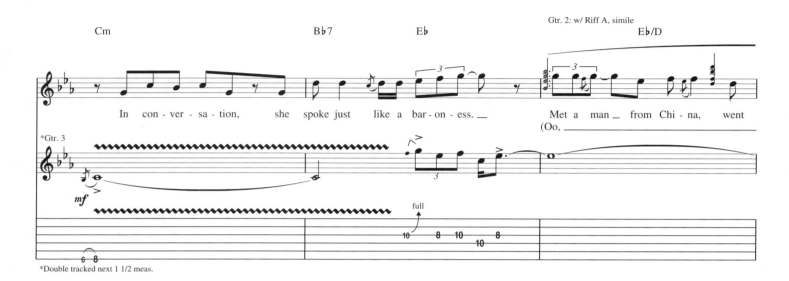

In con - ver - sa - tion, she spoke just like a bar - on - ess. ___ Met a man __ from Chi - na, went (Oo, ___

*Gtr. 3

*Double tracked next 1 1/2 meas.

down to Gei - sha Mi - nah, then a - gain in - ci - den - t'ly if you're
a kill - er, kill - er, she's a

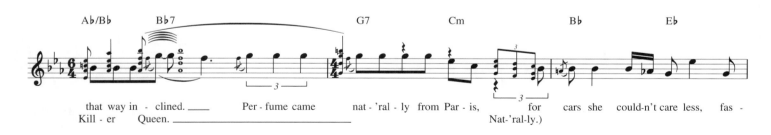

that way in - clined. ___ Per - fume came nat - 'ral - ly from Par - is, for cars she could-n't care less, fas -
Kill - er Queen. ___ Nat.'ral-ly.)

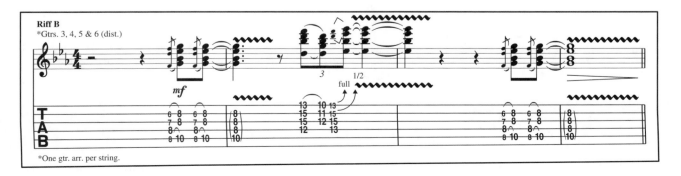

Riff B
*Gtrs. 3, 4, 5 & 6 (dist.)

*One gtr. arr. per string.

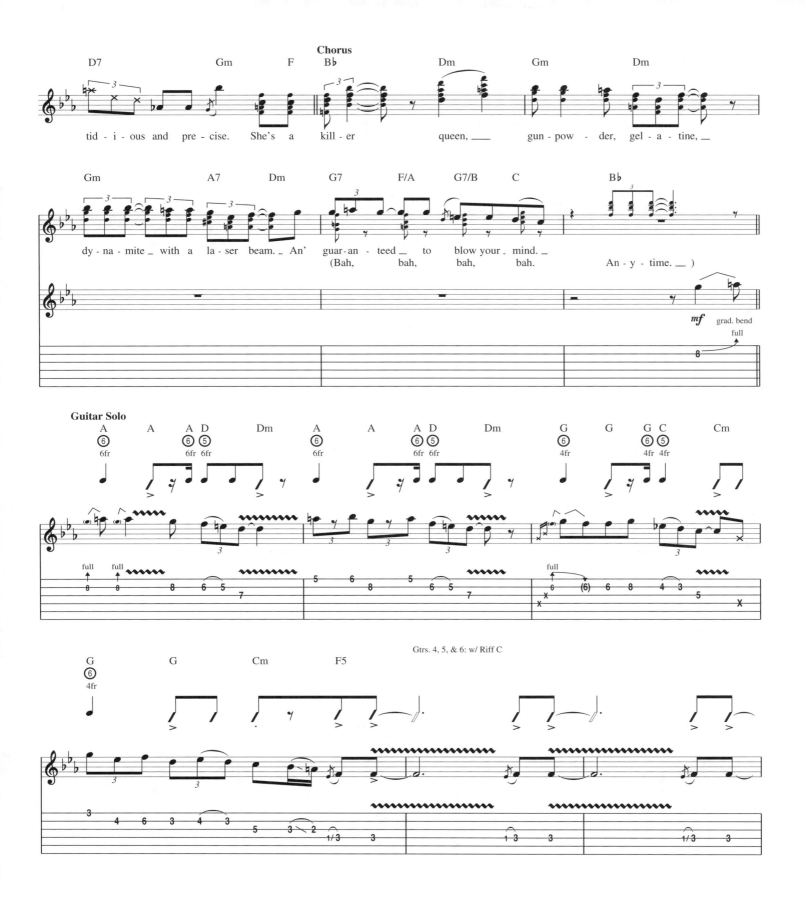

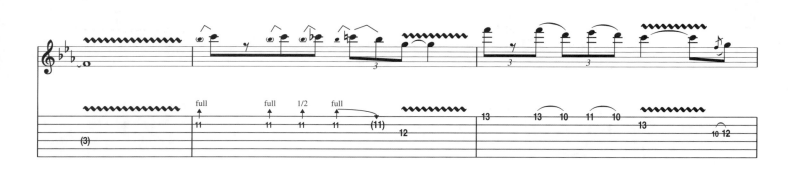

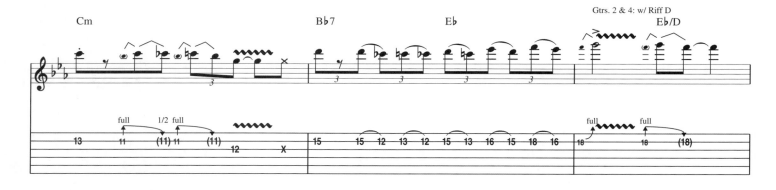

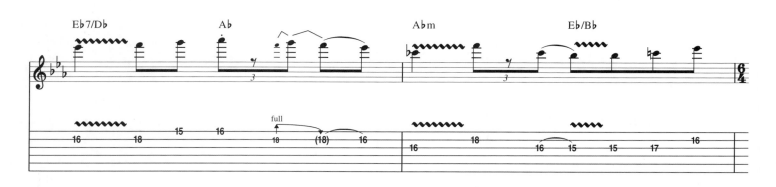

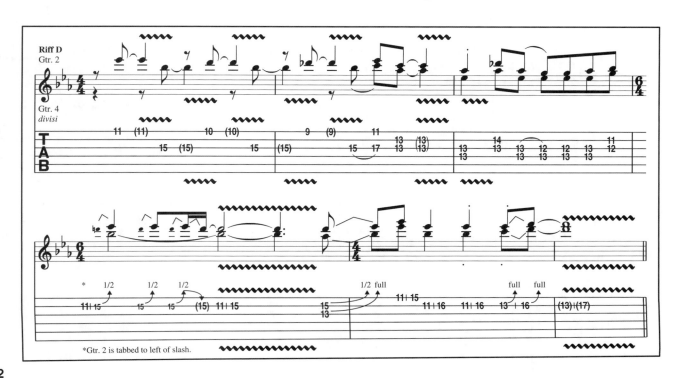

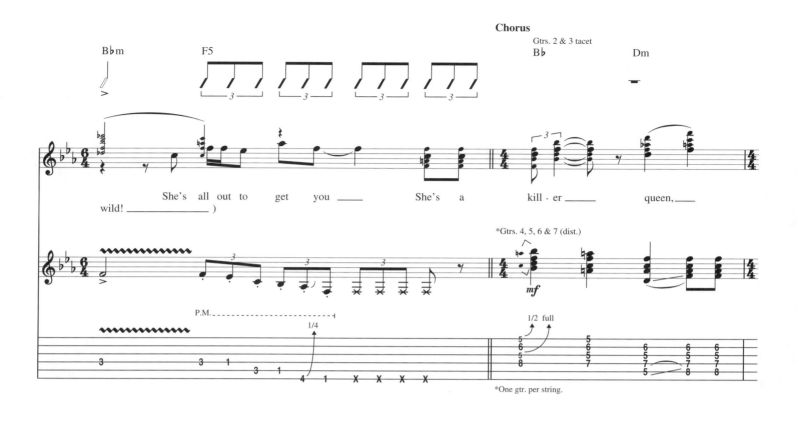

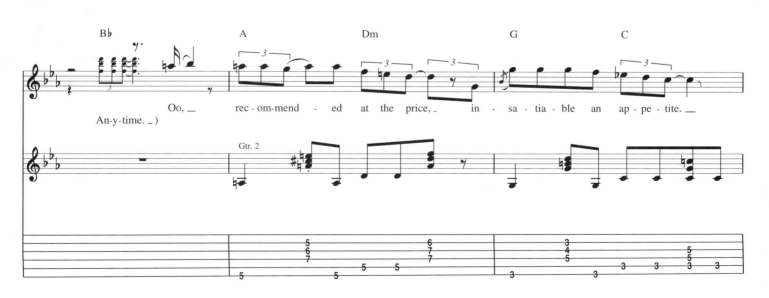

Laid to Rest

Words and Music by Chris Adler, David Blythe, John Campbell, Mark Morton and Will Adler

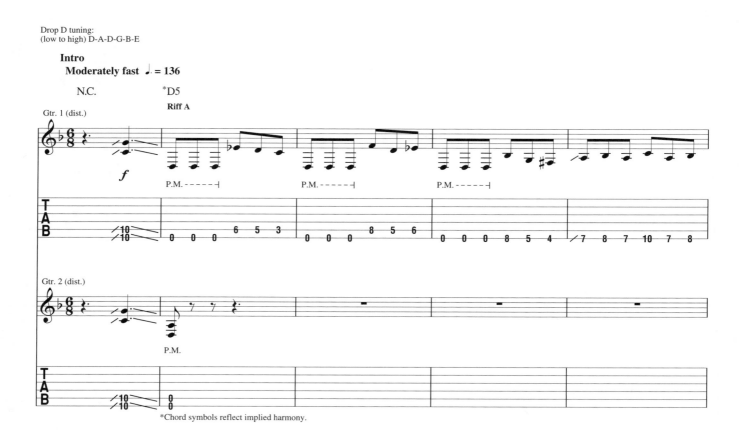

*Chord symbols reflect implied harmony.

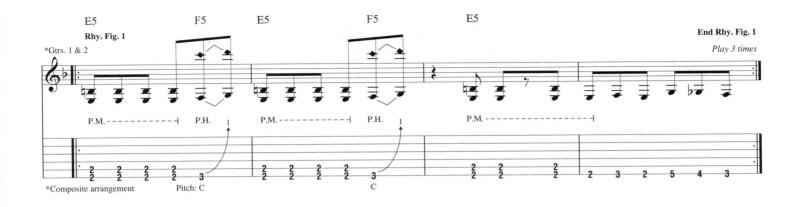

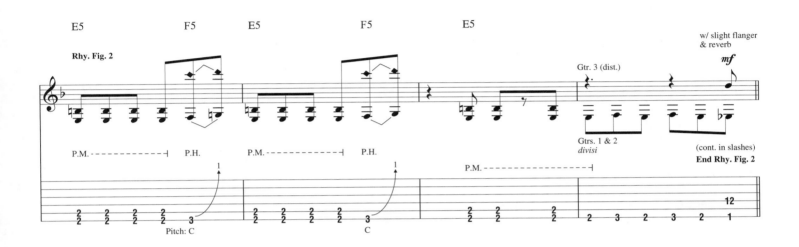

Verse
Half-time feel

1. If there was a sin-gle day I could

live,

a sin-gle breath I could take,

I'd   trade ___ all   the   oth - ers   a - way.

Gtr. 3

let ring - - - - - - - - - -

Interlude

Gtrs. 1 & 2: w/ Rhy. Fig. 1

𝄋

Gtr. 3 tacet

Gtrs. 1 & 2: w/ Rhy. Fig. 2

E5   F5   E5   F5   E5   F5   E5   F5   E5

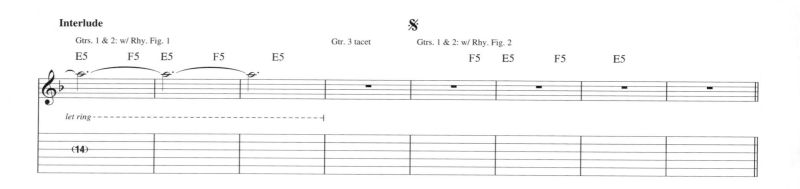

let ring -

(14)

Verse

Gtr. 1: w/ Riff A (2 times)
Gtr. 2: w/ Riff A (4 times)

D5

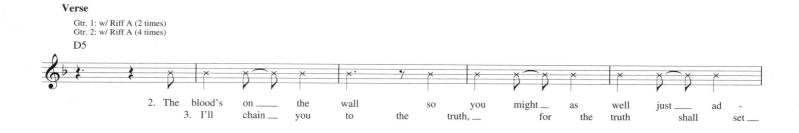

2. The   blood's   on ___ the   wall   so   you   might ___ as   well   just ___ ad -
3. I'll   chain ___ you   to   the   truth, ___   for   the   truth   shall   set ___

mit   it, ___   and   bleach   out ___ the   stains,   com -
___ you ___ free. ___   I'll   turn ___ the   screws   of   ven -

mit   to ___   for - get - ting ___ it.
- geance   and   bur - y ___ you ___ with   hon - es - ty. ___

Chorus

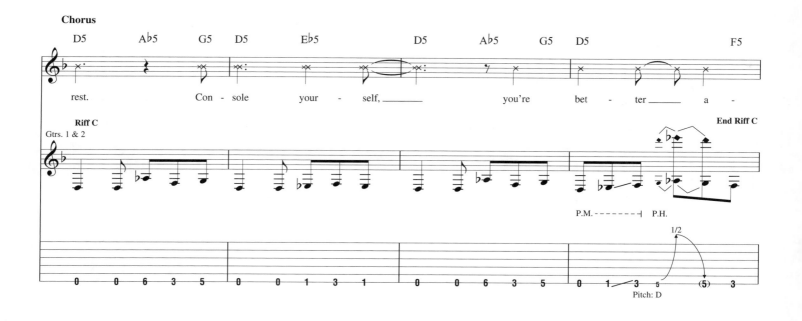

rest. Con - sole your - self, ____ you're bet - ter a -

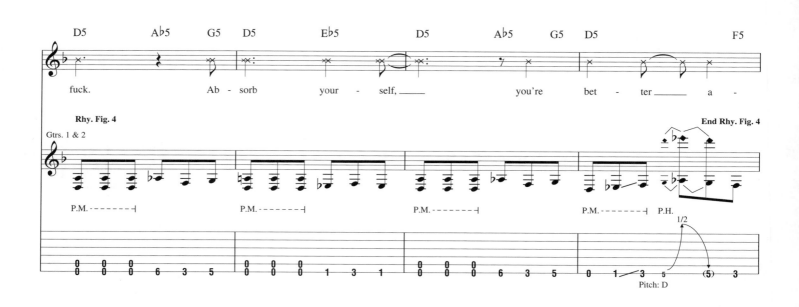

lone. De - stroy your - self, ____ see who gives ____ a

fuck. Ab - sorb your - self, ____ you're bet - ter a -

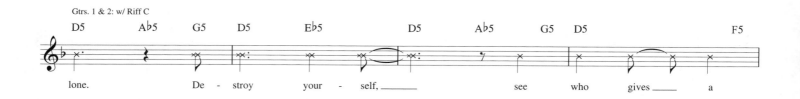

To Coda ⊕   *D.S. al Coda*

Interlude

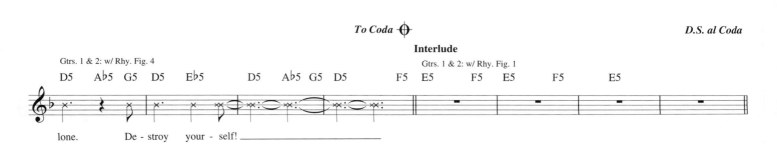

lone. De - stroy your - self! _____

⊕ Coda

Bridge

Eb5

Gtrs. 1 & 2

P.M. -

N.C.

See __ who gives a fuck.

P.M. -

Half-time feel

Gtrs. 1 & 2: w/ Rhy. Fig. 3 (4 times)

D5

See __ who gives a

fuck.   See __ who gives a

Interlude

Gtr. 1: w/ Riff A (1st 4 meas.)   Gtr. 1: w/ Riff A (1st 4 meas.)
Gtr. 2: w/ Rhy. Fig. 3   Gtr. 2: w/ Rhy. Fig. 3

D5

fuck.

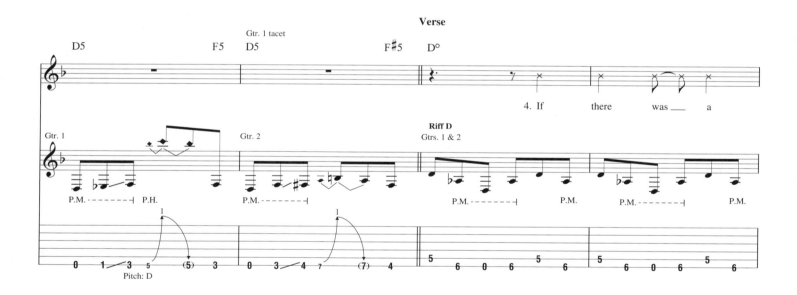

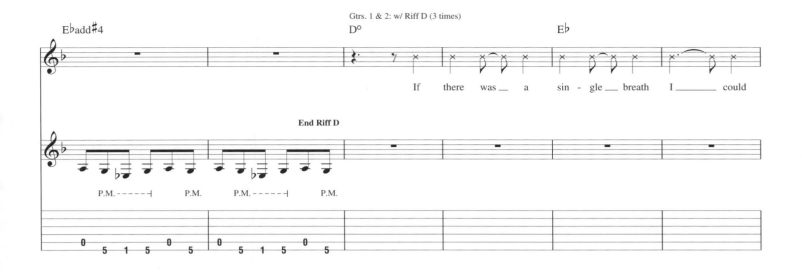

Gtrs. 1 & 2: w/ Riff D (3 times)

If there was ___ a sin - gle ___ breath I ___ could

End Riff D

P.M. ------| P.M. P.M. ------| P.M.

take, I'd trade all ___ the

oth - ers ___ a - way. ___

I'd trade all ___ the oth - ers ___ a - way.

Outro

Half-time feel

Gtrs. 1 & 2: w/ Rhy. Fig. 3
Gtr. 3: w/ Riff B

Play 3 times

Gtrs. 1 & 2: w/ Rhy. Fig. 3

Gtr. 3

let ring ------

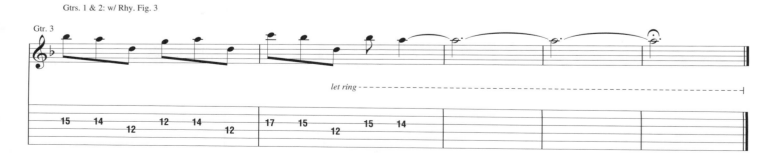

Last Child

Words and Music by Steven Tyler and Brad Whitford

____ stand ___ up ___ on my feet in the cit-y,
____ in the cit-y and my loves in the mead-ow,

got ___
hands ___

____ to get back ___ to the real nit-ty grit-ty.
____ on the plough ___ and my feet's in the ghet-to.

Pre-Chorus

A9   A13   A9   Ab9   A9   A13   Ab9

Gtr. 3

Yes sir, no sir, don't come close to my home ___ sweet home, can't catch no dose from a hot ___
Stand up, sit down, don't do noth-in' it ain't ___ no good when boss man's stuf-fin' it down ___

Gtr. 1

Gtr. 2

Gtr. 4
divisi

*

* Gtr. 4 tabbed to the right of slash.

156

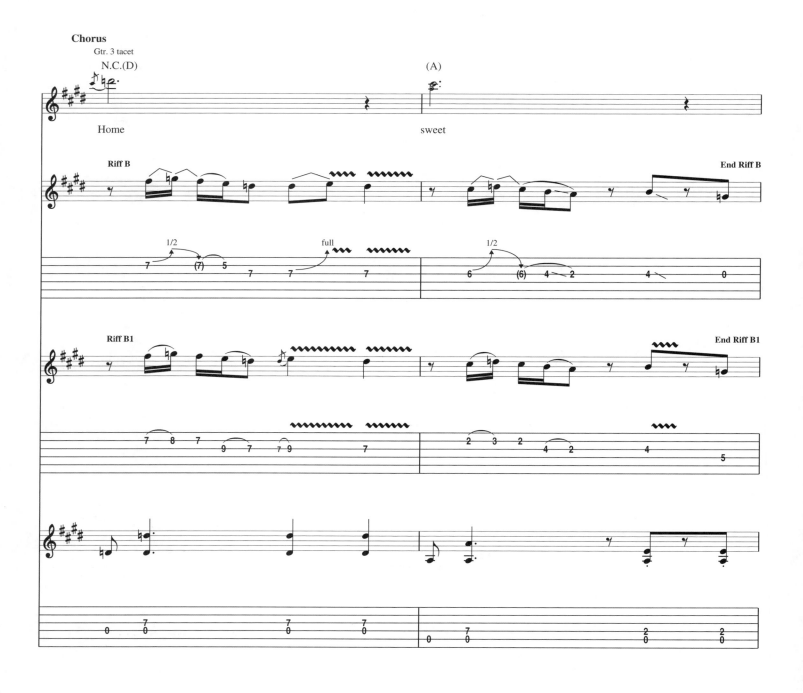

Chorus

Gtr. 3 tacet

Home sweet

Riff B ... *End Riff B*

Riff B1 ... *End Riff B1*

Gtr. 1: w/ Riff A
Gtrs. 3 & 4: w/ Rhy. Figs. 1 & 1A

E9

home. 2. Get out

Gtr. 2

Madhouse

Words and Music by Joe Bellardini, Frank Bello, Charles Benante, Scott Ian Rosenfeld and Dan Spitz

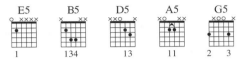

Spoken: It's time for your medication, Mister Brown. (Maniacal laughter:) Ooh, hoo, ha, ha, ha...

Message in a Bottle

Music and Lyrics by Sting

Pre-Chorus

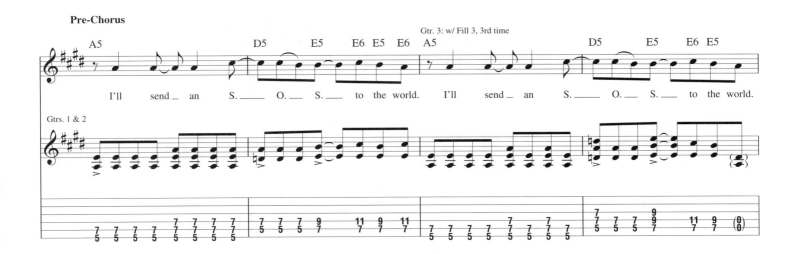

I'll send an S. O. S. to the world. I'll send an S. O. S. to the world.

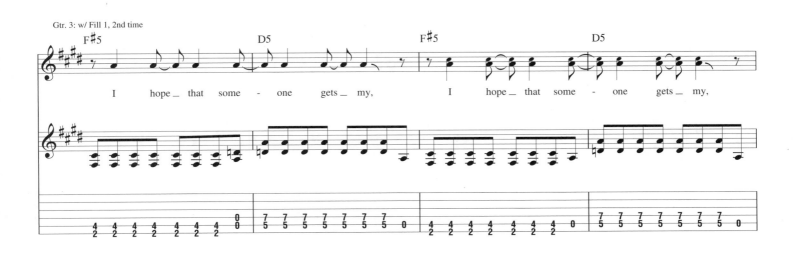

I hope that some - one gets my, I hope that some - one gets my,

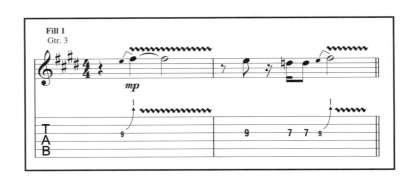

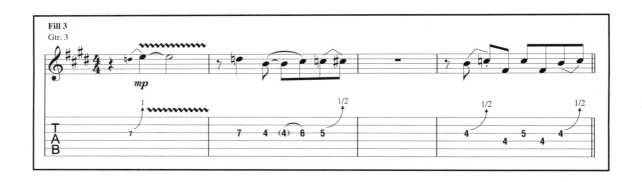

To Coda ⊕ **Chorus**

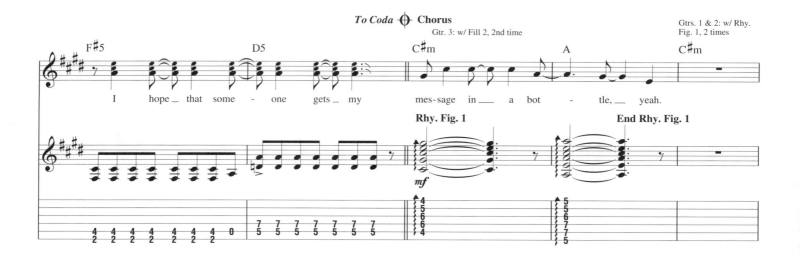

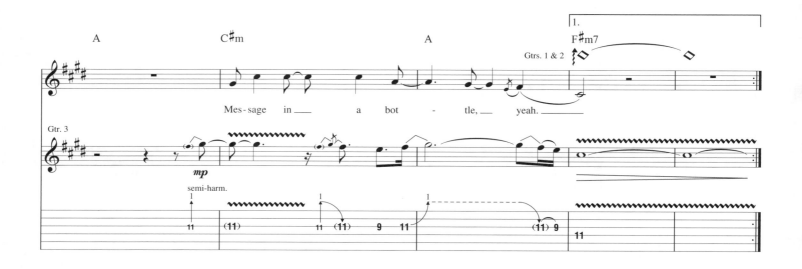

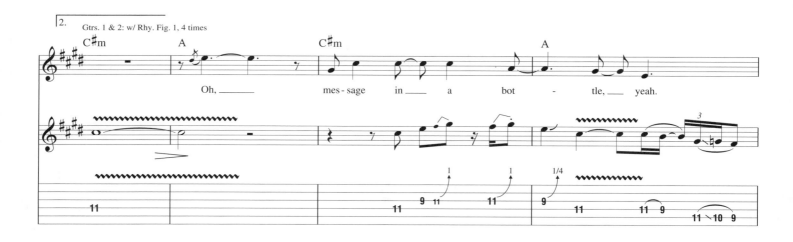

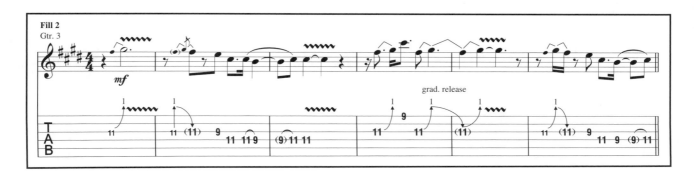

168

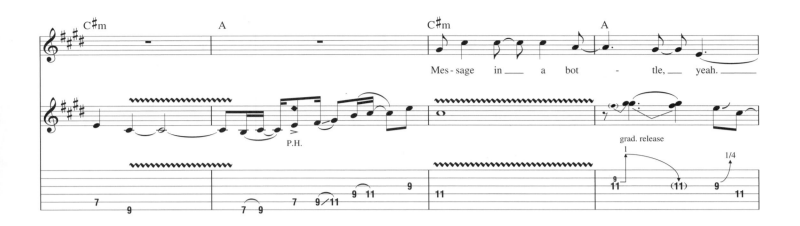

D.S. al Coda

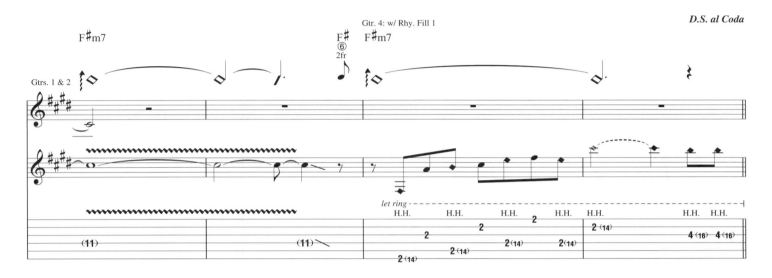

Coda

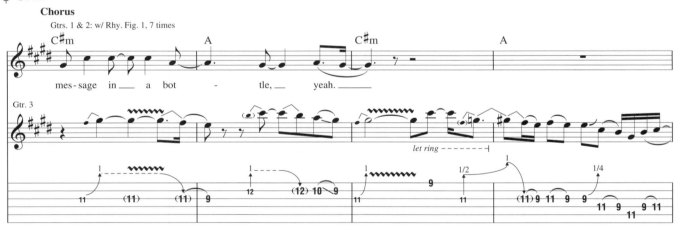

169

Additional Lyrics

Woke up this morning,
I don't believe what I saw.
Hundred billion bottles washed up on the shore.
Seems I never noticed being alone.
Hundred billion castaways,
Looking for a home.

Monkey Wrench

Words and Music by David Grohl, Nate Mendel and Pat Smear

172

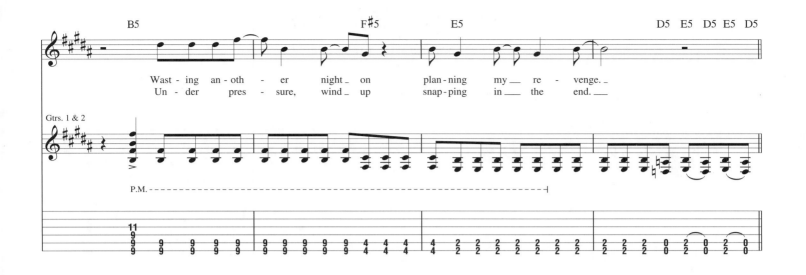

Wast - ing an - oth - er night on plan - ning my re - venge.
Un - der pres - sure, wind up snap - ping in the end.

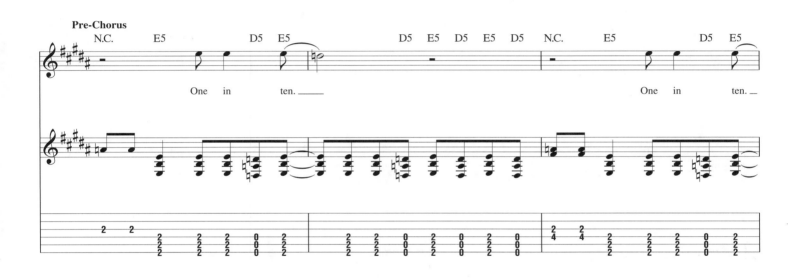

Pre-Chorus

One in ten.

One in ten.

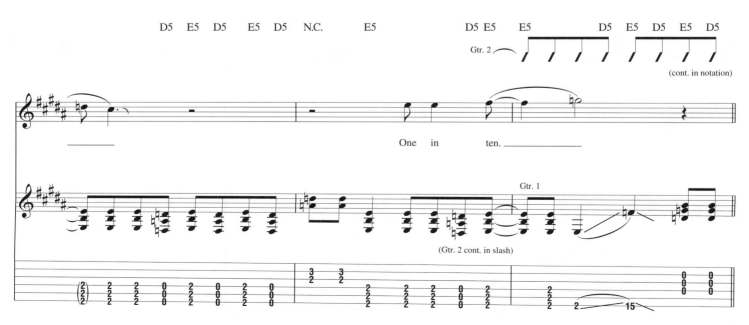

One in ten.

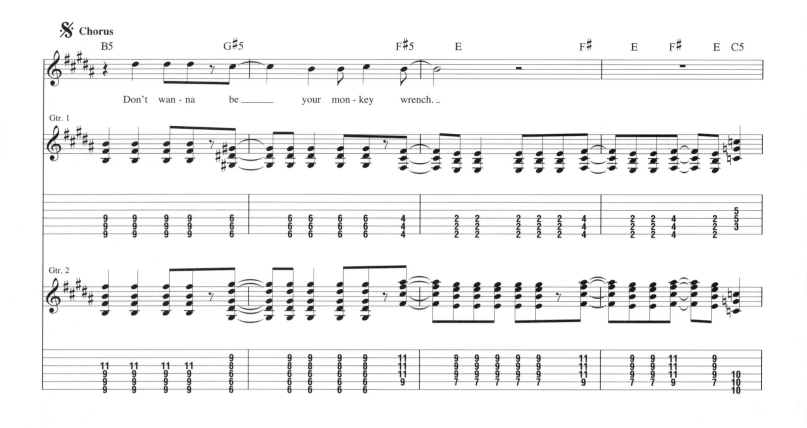

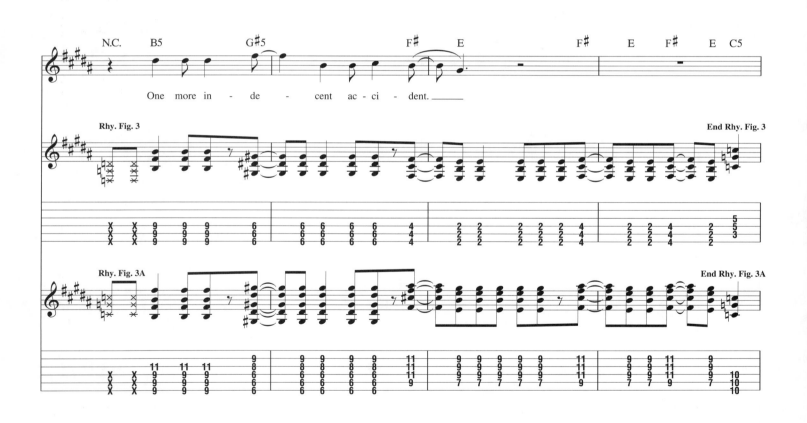

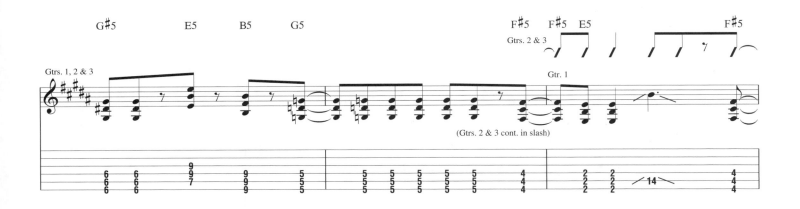

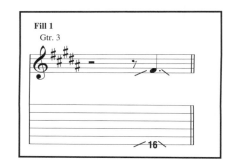

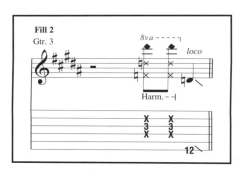

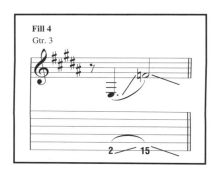

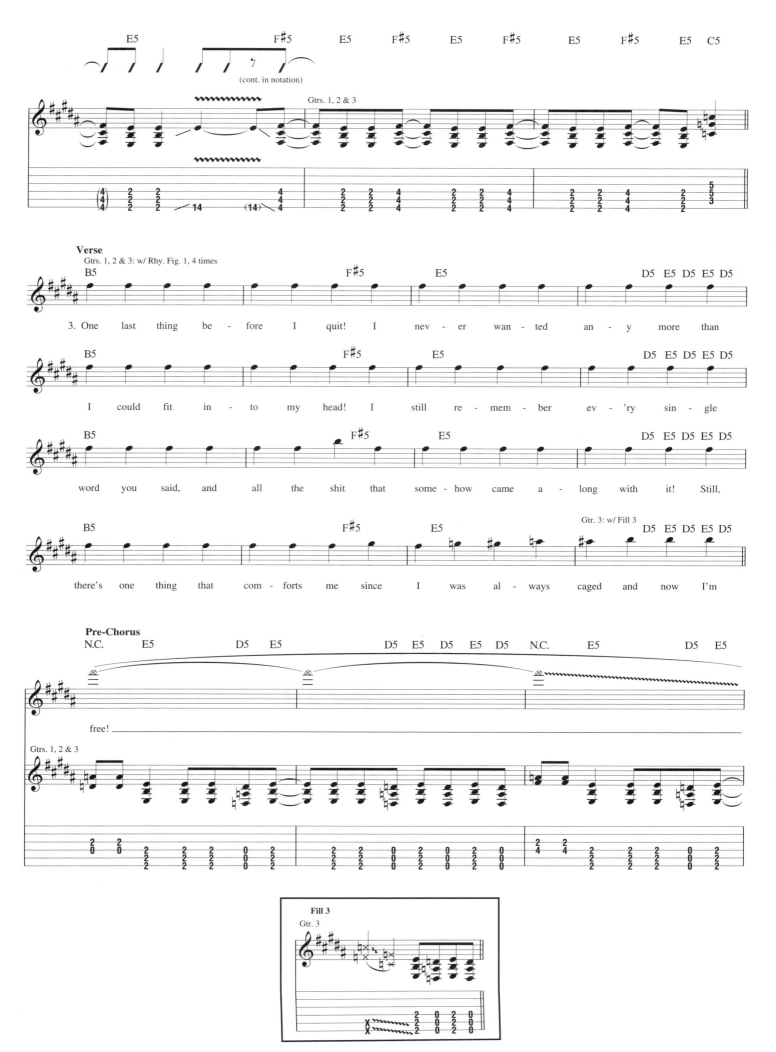

Verse

3. One last thing before I quit! I never wanted any more than
I could fit into my head! I still remember ev'ry single
word you said, and all the shit that somehow came along with it! Still,
there's one thing that comforts me since I was always caged and now I'm

Pre-Chorus

free!

Fill 3
Gtr. 3

More Than a Feeling

Words and Music by Tom Scholz

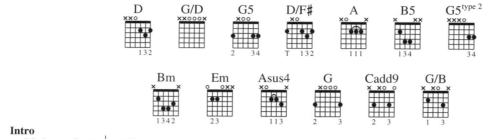

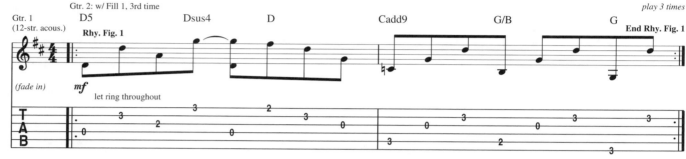

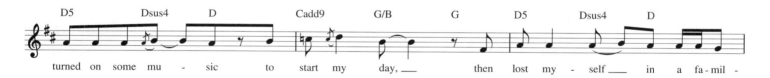

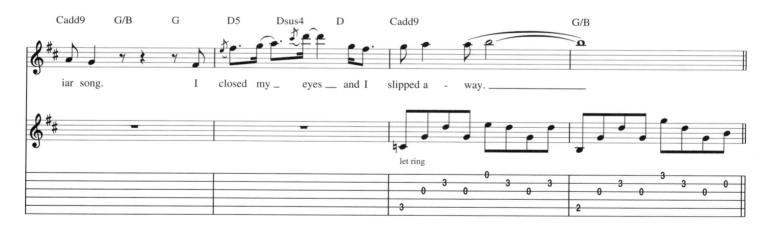

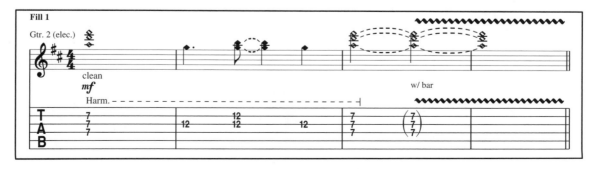

3. When I'm tired __ and think-in' cold, I hide in my mu - sic, for-get the __ day. __ And

dream of a girl __ I used to know, __ I close my __ eyes __ and she slipped a - way. __

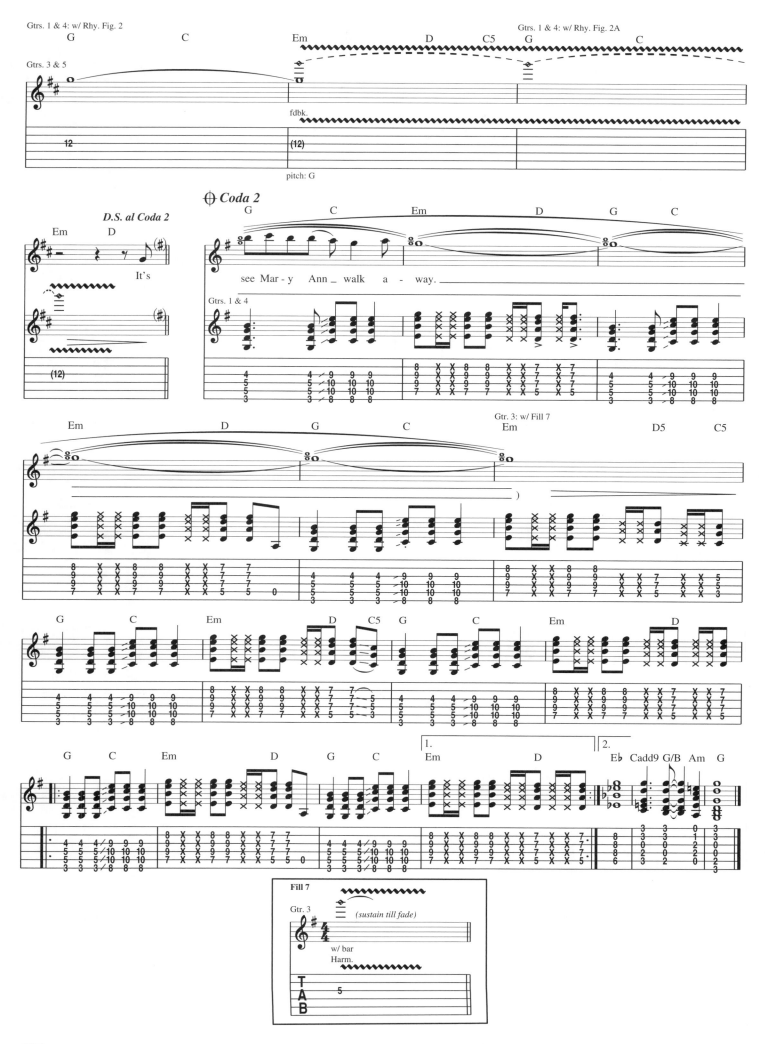

see Mar - y Ann _ walk a - way.

Mother

Words and Music by Glenn Danzig

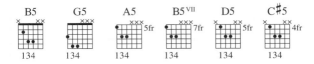

Verse

2. Moth-er, ___ can you keep them in the dark for life? ___ Can you hide them from the
3. Moth-er, ___ tell your chil-dren not to hold my ___ hand. ___ Tell your chil-dren not to

wait-ing world? ___ Oh, ___ moth-er. ___
un-der-stand. ___ Oh, ___ moth-er. ___

Fa-ther, ___ gon-na take your daugh-ter out to-night. ___ Gon-na show her
Fa-ther, ___ do you wan-na bang heads with me? ___ Do you wan-na feel

my world. ___ Oh, ___ fa-ther. ___
ev-'ry-thing? ___ Oh, ___ fa-ther. ___

Rhy. Fill 1

189

Possum Kingdom

Words and Music by Todd Lewis

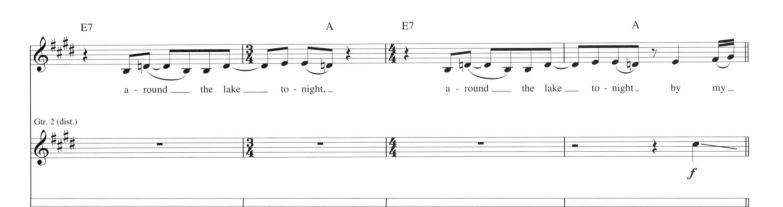

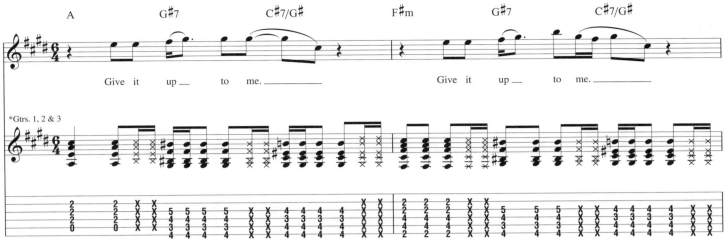

*Gtrs. 1, 2 & 3

*Composite arrangement

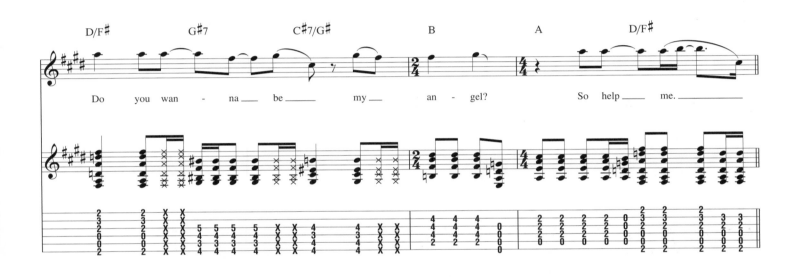

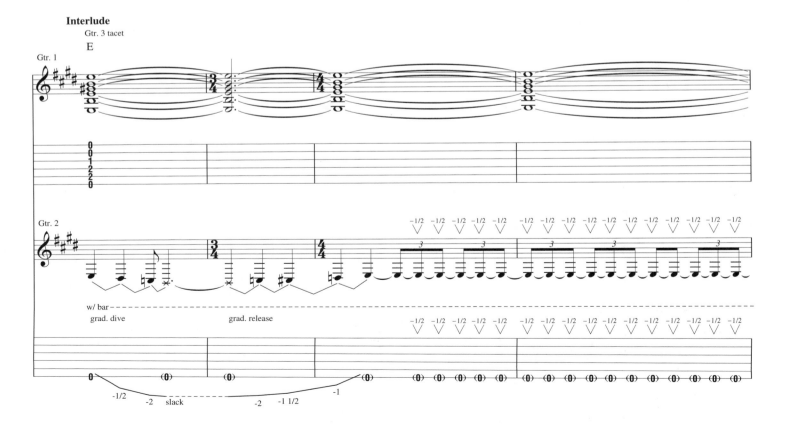

Interlude

Gtr. 3 tacet

Gtr. 1

Gtr. 2

w/ bar---

grad. dive   grad. release

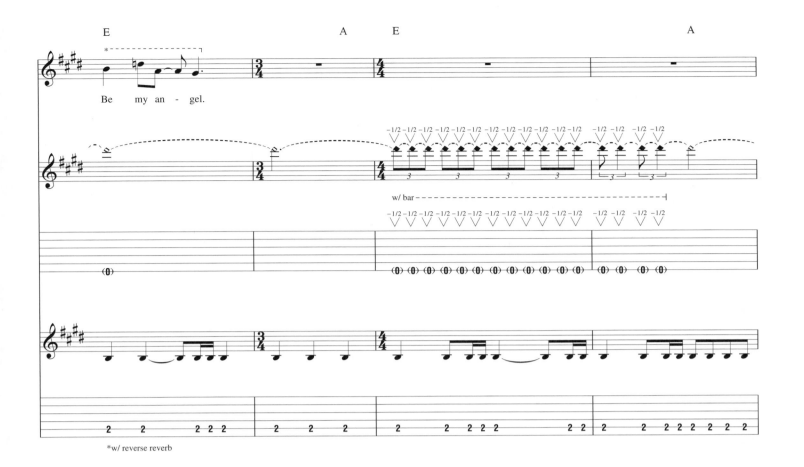

*w/ reverse reverb

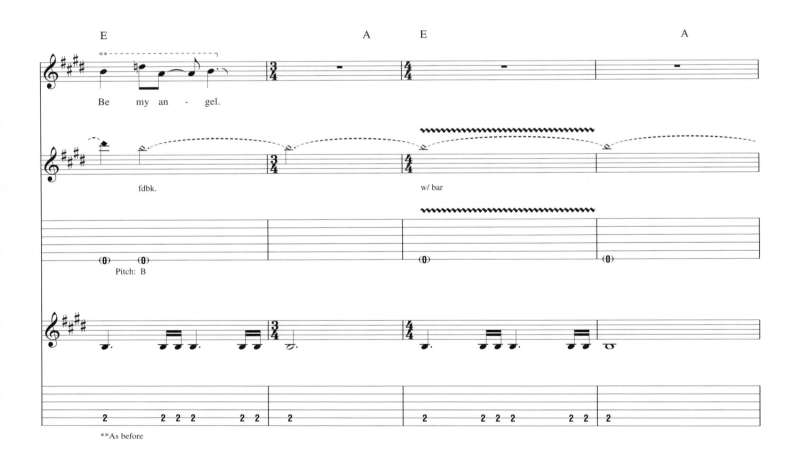

**As before

*w/ reverse reverb, next 8 meas.

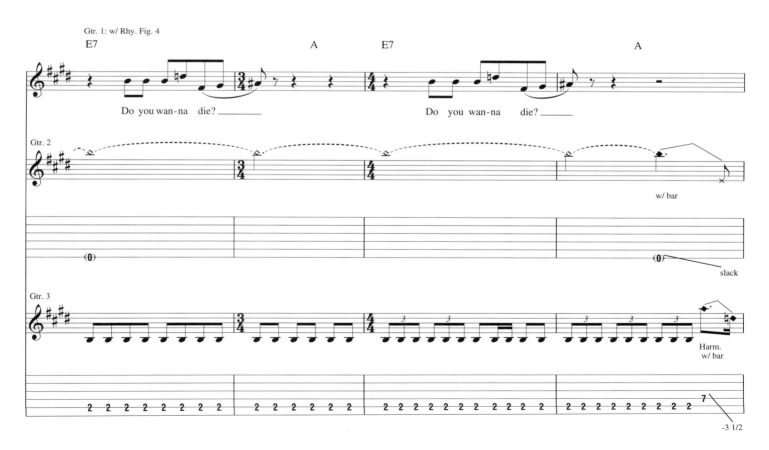

Rock and Roll Hoochie Koo

Words and Music by Rick Derringer

Intro

Moderate Rock ♩ = 100

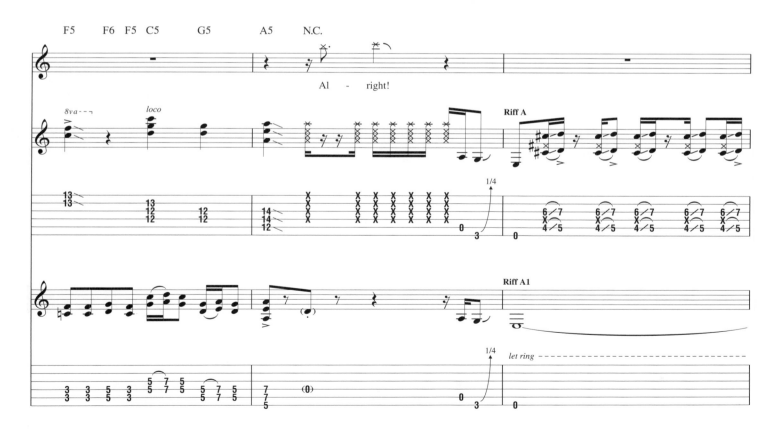

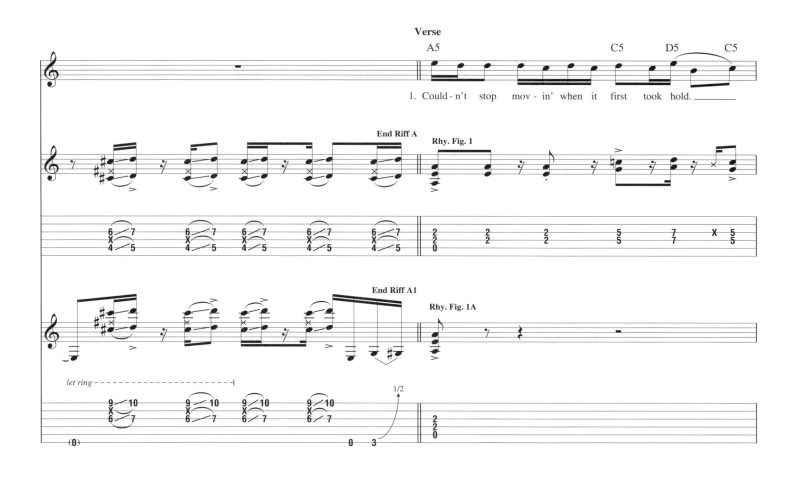

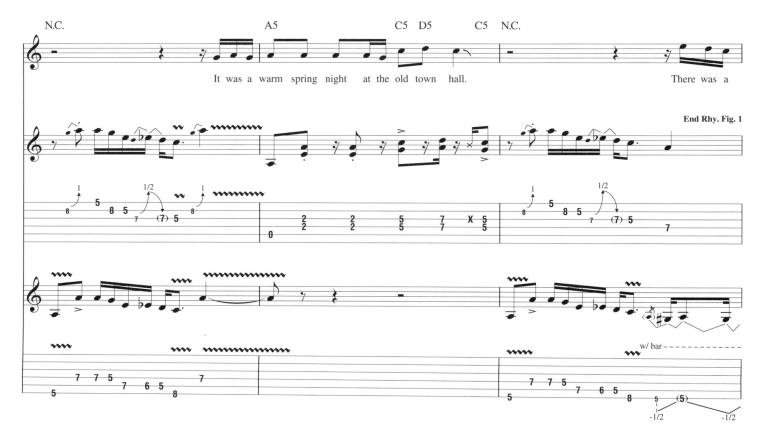

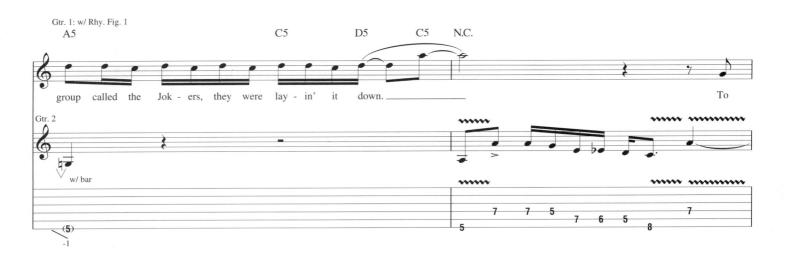

group called the Jok-ers, they were lay-in' it down. _____ To

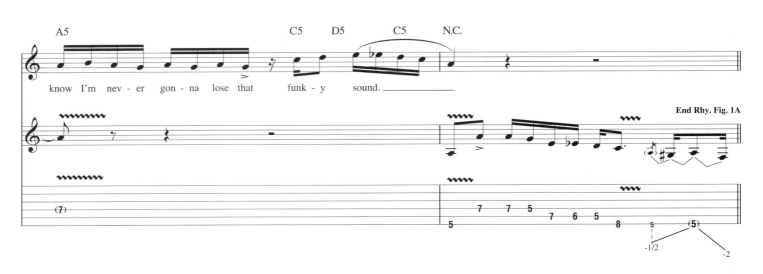

know I'm nev-er gon-na lose that funk-y sound. _____

Chorus

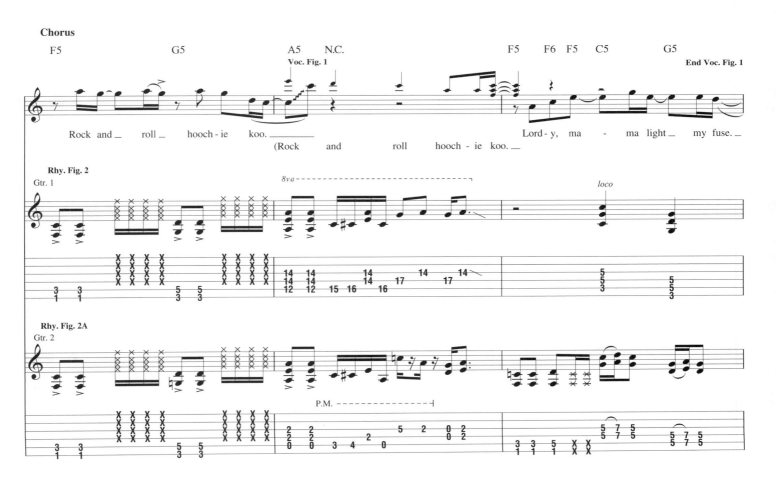

Rock and __ roll __ hooch-ie koo. _____ Lord-y, ma - ma light __ my fuse. __
(Rock and roll hooch-ie koo. __

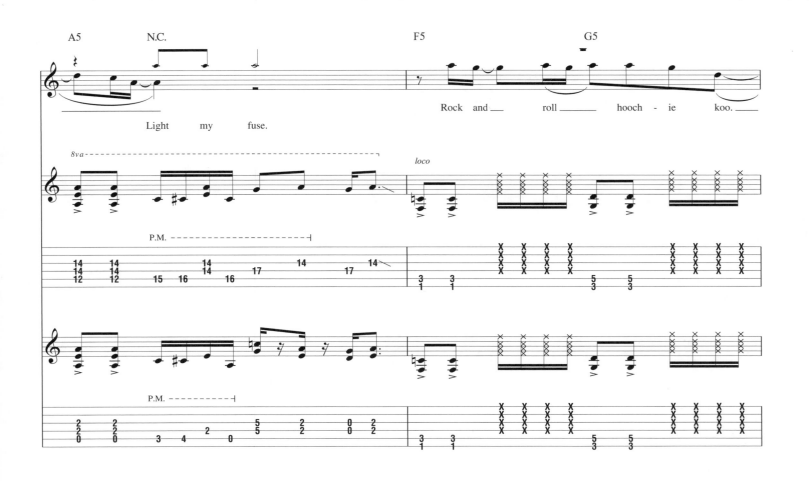

Light my fuse.

Rock and __ roll __ hooch - ie koo. __

Rock and roll hooch - ie koo.) __

Drop on __ out __ an' spread __ the news. __

End Rhy. Fig. 2

End Rhy. Fig. 2A

2. Mos -

%. Verse

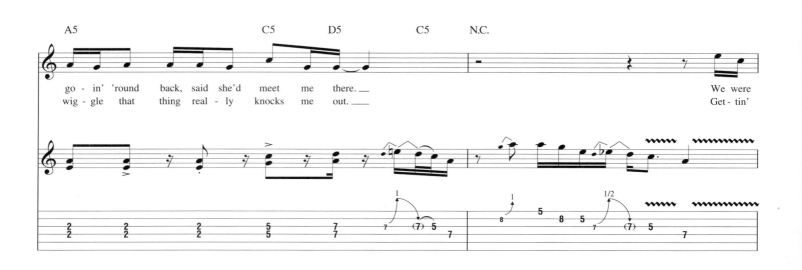

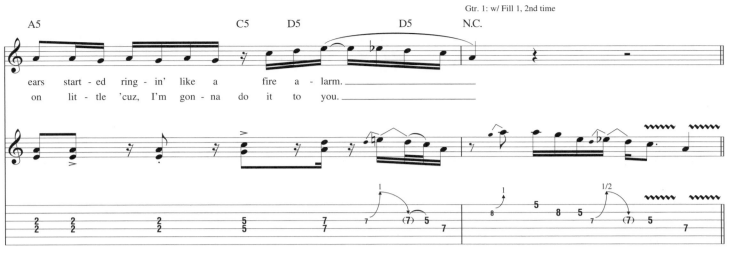

ears start-ed ring-in' like a fire a-larm. _____
on lit-tle 'cuz, I'm gon-na do it to you. _____

Chorus

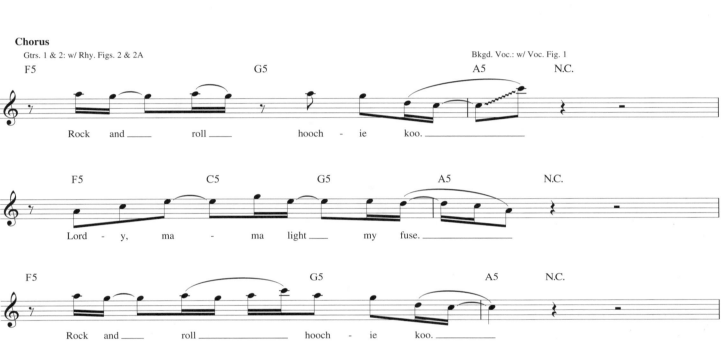

Rock and _____ roll _____ hooch - ie koo. _____

Lord - y, ma - ma light _____ my fuse. _____

Rock and _____ roll _____ hooch - ie koo. _____

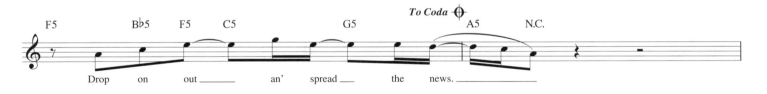

Drop on out _____ an' spread _____ the news. _____

Yeah, some - bod - y said "Keep on rock - in'." Ow! _____

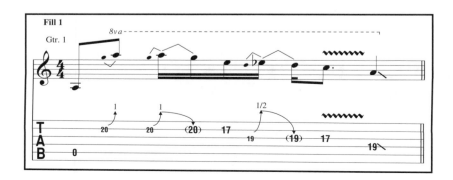

Guitar Solo

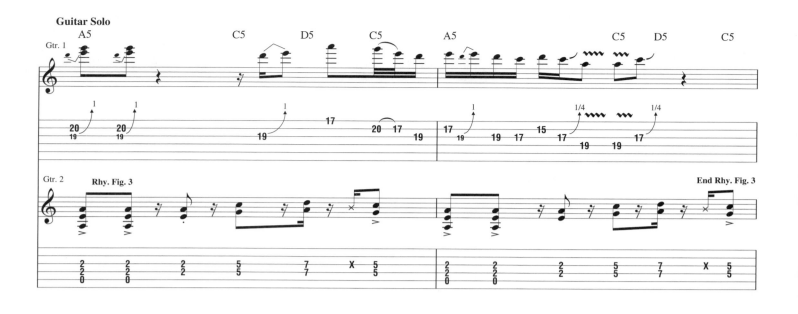

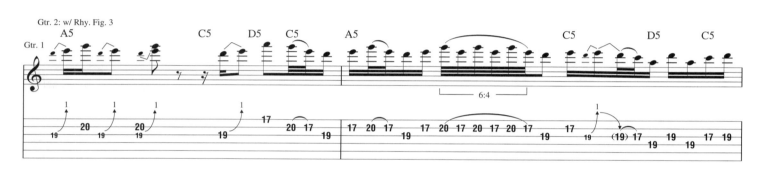

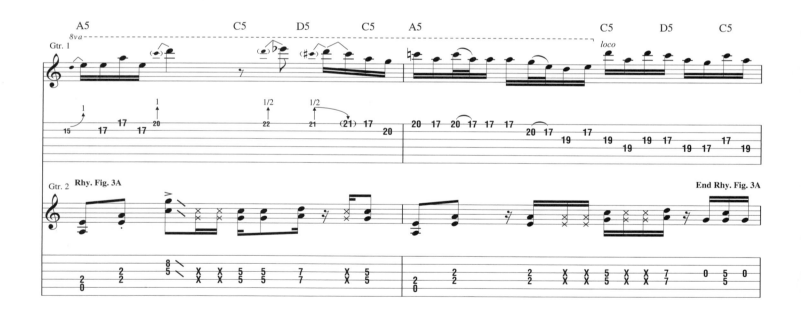

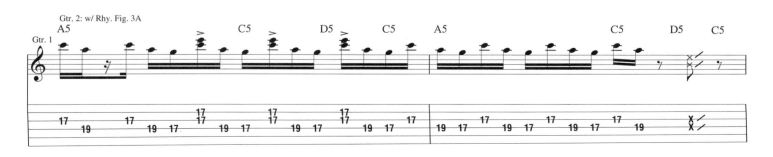

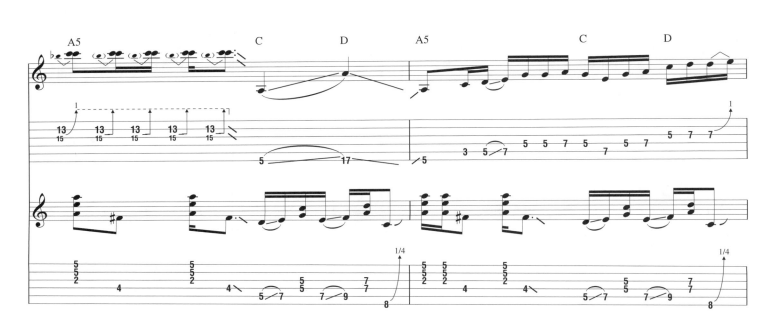

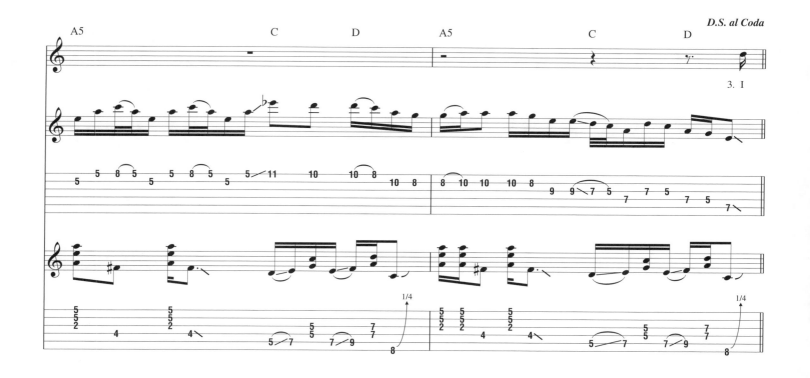

Coda

Outro-Chorus

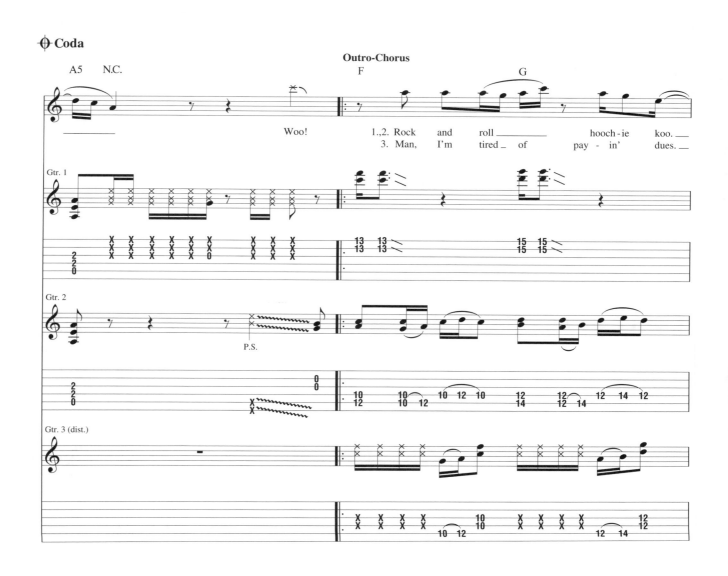

Woo!

1.,2. Rock and roll _____ hooch-ie koo. __

3. Man, I'm tired __ of pay - in' dues. __

Gtr. 1

Gtr. 2

P.S.

Gtr. 3 (dist.)

Lord - y ma - ma, light my fuse.
Dropped on out _____ and spread the news. _____
Done said good-bye _____ to all ___ my blues. _____
Yeah.

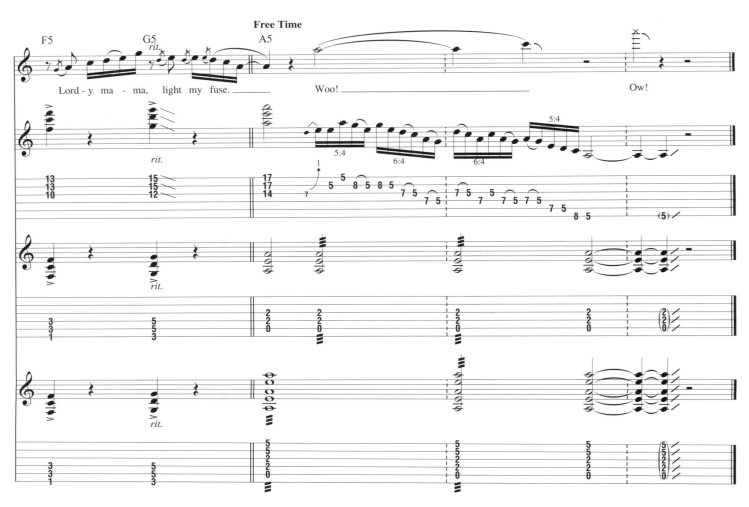

Lord - y ma - ma, light my fuse. _____
Woo! _____
Ow!

Rock This Town

Words and Music by Brian Setzer

Tune down 1/4 step

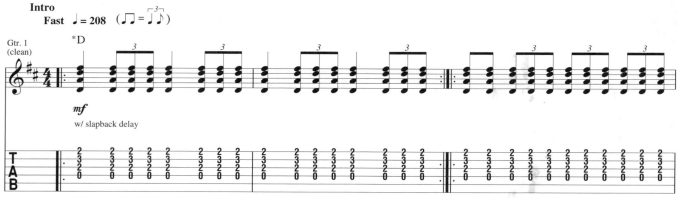

*Chord symbols reflect basic harmony.

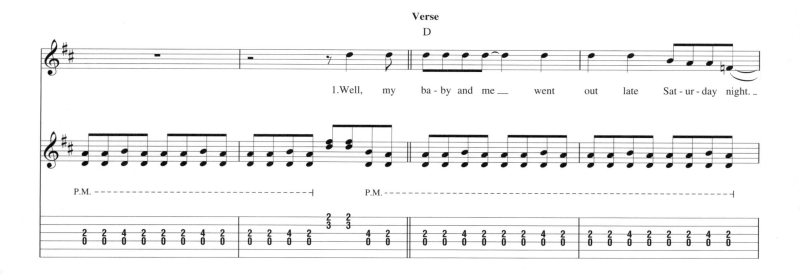

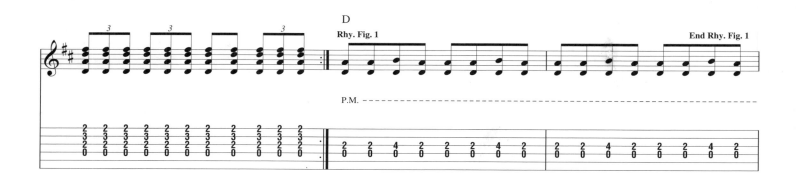

1.Well, my ba-by and me ___ went out late Sat-ur-day night.

Gtr. 1: w/ Rhy. Fig. 1 (2 times)

___ I had my hair piled tight and my ba-by just looked ___ so right. ___

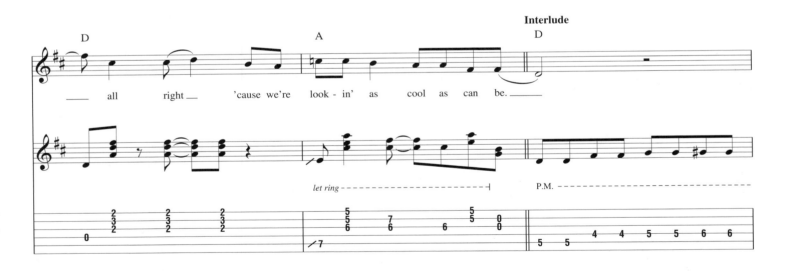

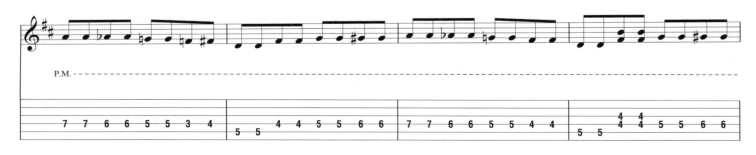

2. Well, we

Verse
D

found a lit - tle place that real - ly did - n't look half bad. ___

I had a whis - key on the rocks and change ___ of a dol - lar for the

A   D

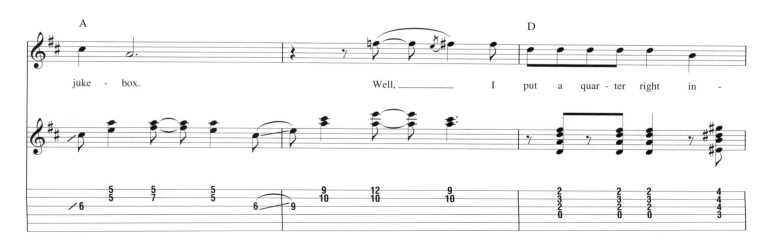

juke - box.   Well, ___ I put a quar - ter right in -

to that can, ___ but all it played was dis - co, man. Come on, ___

___ pret - ty ba - by, let's get out of here right a - way. ___

We're gon - na

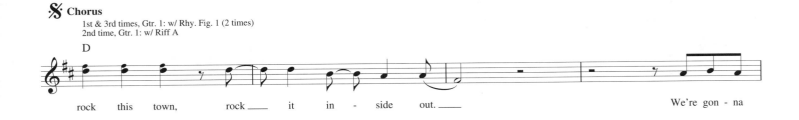

𝄋 **Chorus**
1st & 3rd times, Gtr. 1: w/ Rhy. Fig. 1 (2 times)
2nd time, Gtr. 1: w/ Riff A

rock this town, rock ___ it in - side out. ___

We're gon - na

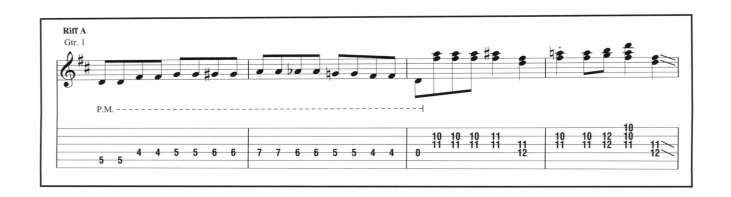

rock this town, make ___ 'em scream ___ and shout. _____

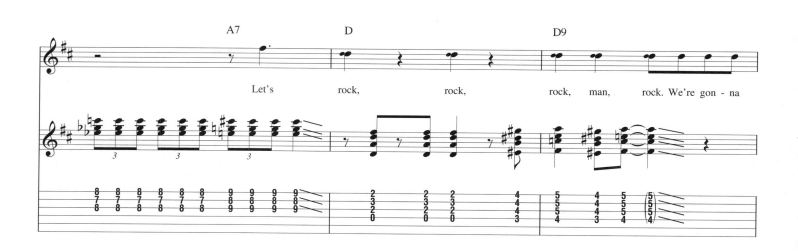

Let's rock, rock, rock, man, rock. We're gon-na

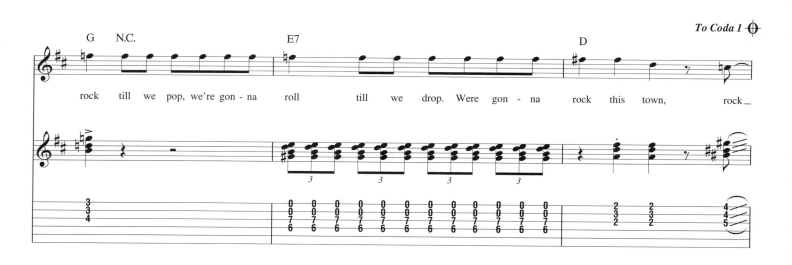

rock till we pop, we're gon-na roll till we drop. Were gon-na rock this town, rock ___

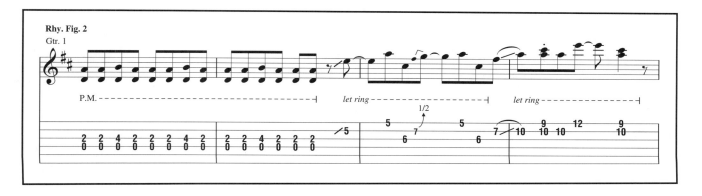

Interlude

Woo!

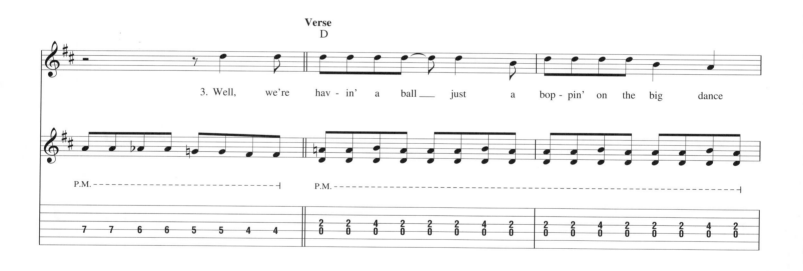

Verse

3. Well, we're hav - in' a ball ___ just a bop - pin' on the big dance

floor. ___

Well, there's a real square cat; he looks of

Guitar Solo

*D

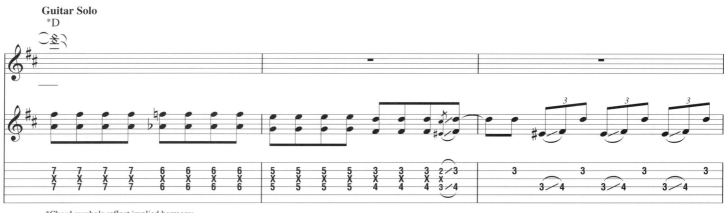

*Chord symbols reflect implied harmony.

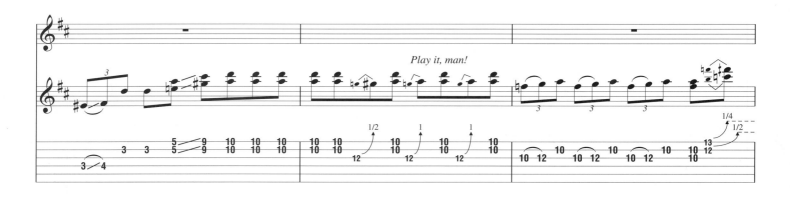

Play it, man!

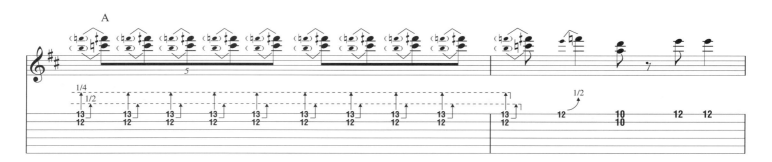

A

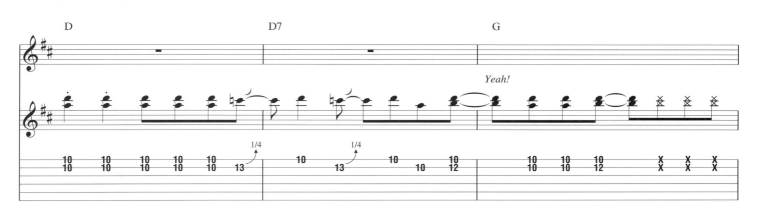

D   D7   G

Yeah!

E7   D   A

1 hold bend

218

Search and Destroy

Words and Music by Iggy Pop and James Williamson

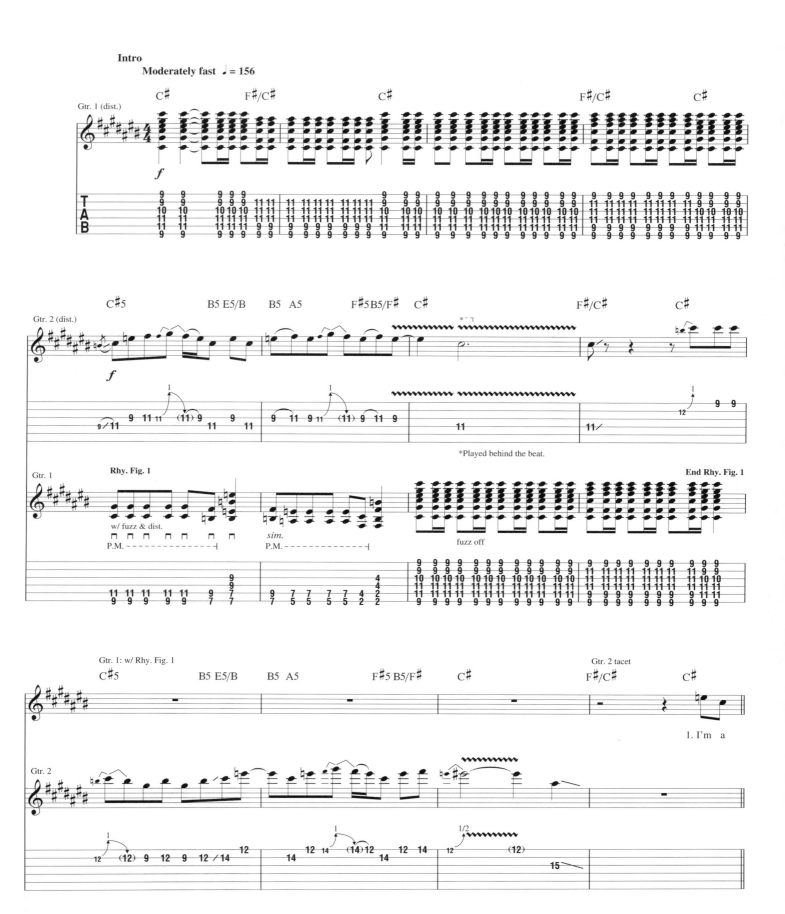

And I'm the world's ___ for - got - ten boy. ___

The one who's search - in', ___ search-in' to de - stroy. ___

And hon - ey, I'm ___ the world's for - got - ten boy. ___

Sharp Dressed Man

Words and Music by Billy F Gibbons, Dusty Hill and Frank Beard

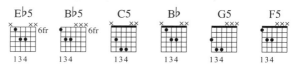

Gtr. 3: Open G tuning:
(low to high) D-G-D-G-B-D

Intro

Moderately fast ♩ = 124

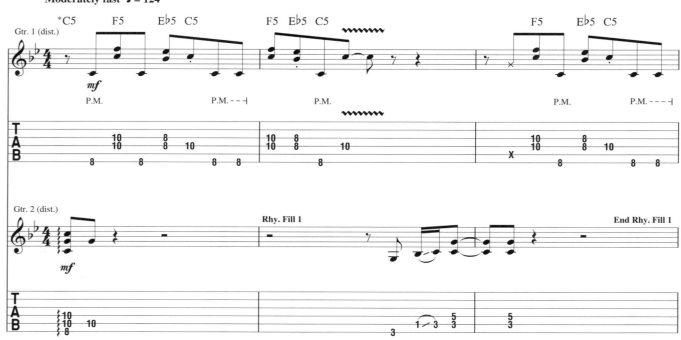

*Chord symbols reflect basic harmony.

Gtr. 2: w/ Rhy. Fill 1 (4 1/2 times)

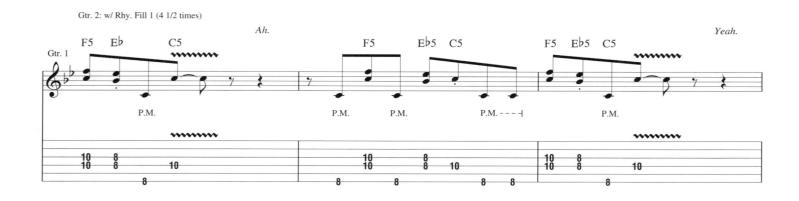

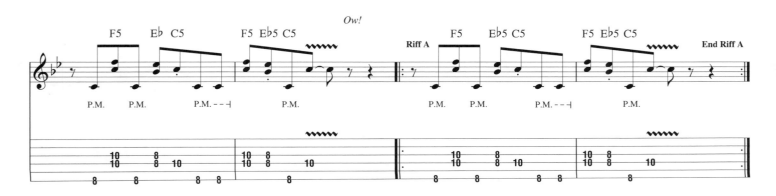

C5   Bb5 I   G5

let ring- - - - -|

Interlude

Gtr. 1: w/ Riff A (4 times)
Gtrs. 2 & 3 tacet

Gtr. 2: w/ Rhy. Fill 2 (3 1/2 times)

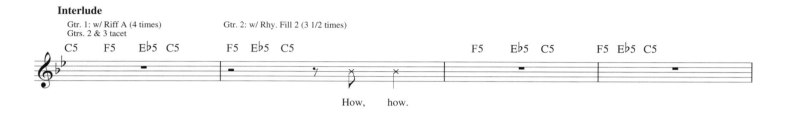

C5   F5   Eb5 C5   F5   Eb5 C5   F5   Eb5 C5   F5   Eb5 C5

How,   how.

D.S. al Coda

F5   Eb5 C5   F5   Eb5 C5   F5   Eb5 C5   F5 Eb5 C5

⊕ **Coda**

Outro-Guitar Solo

Gtr. 2: w/ Rhy. Fill 2 (9 times)

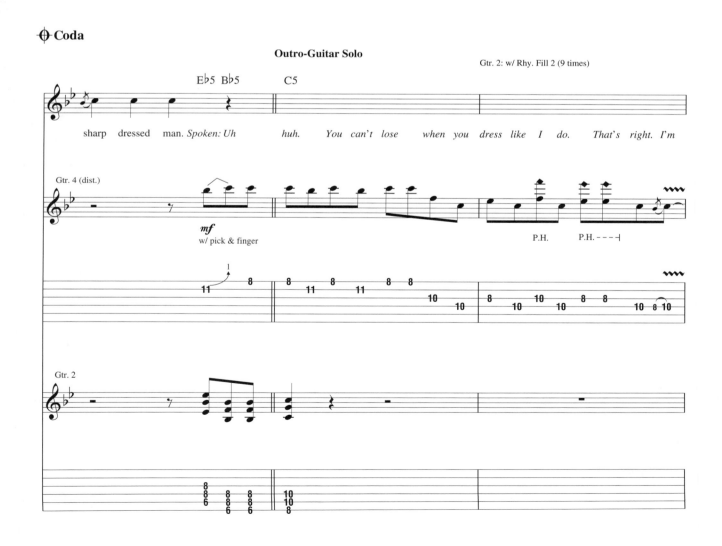

Eb5 Bb5   C5

sharp   dressed   man. *Spoken:* Uh   huh.   You can't lose   when you dress like I   do.   That's right. I'm

Gtr. 4 (dist.)

mf
w/ pick & finger

P.H.   P.H. - - - -|

Gtr. 2

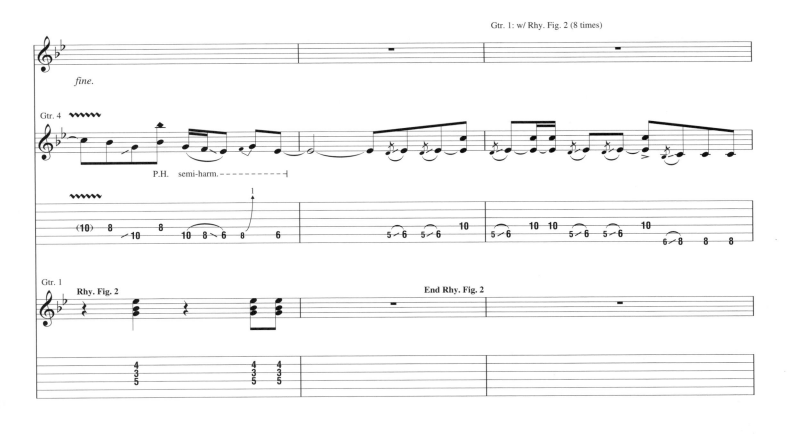

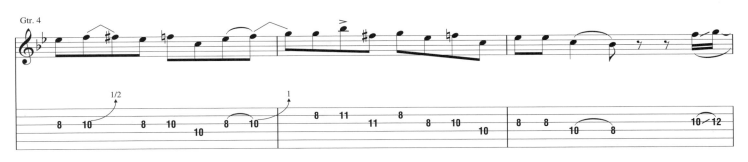

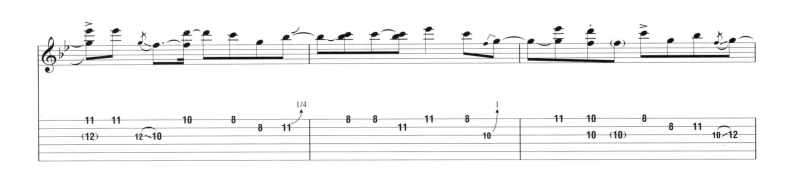

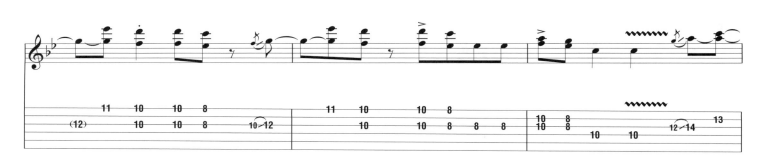

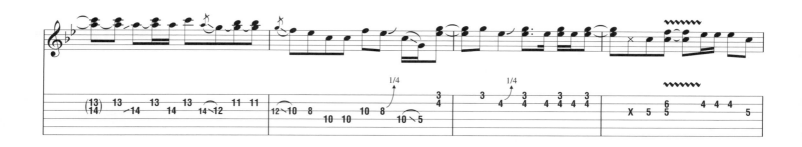

F5

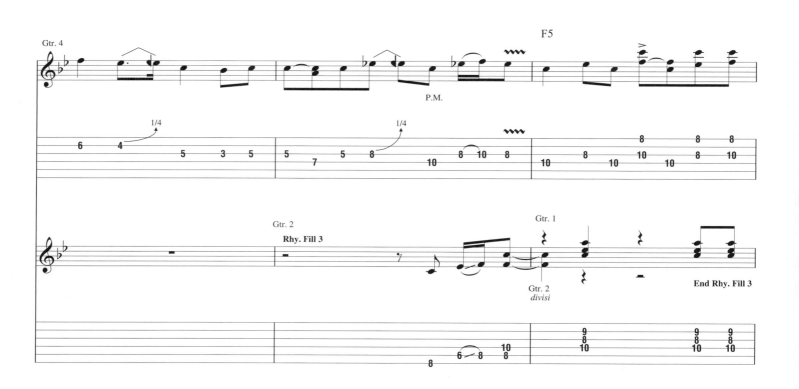

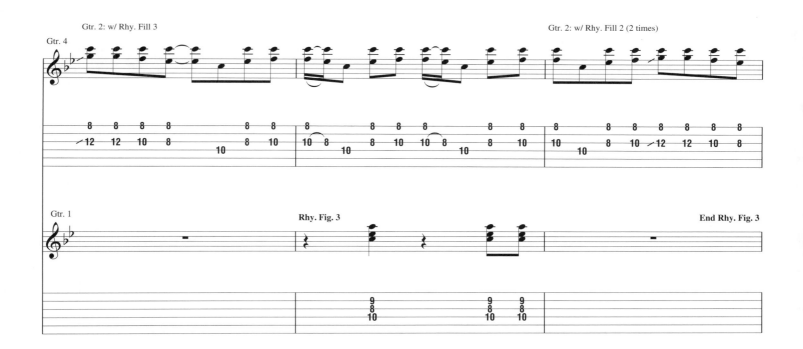

232

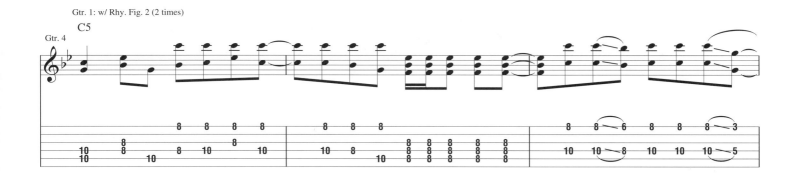

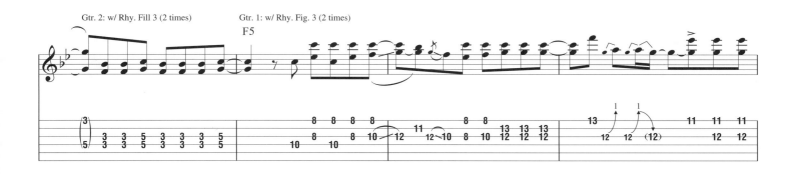

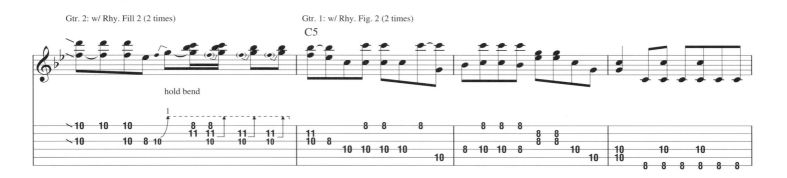

Smoke on the Water

Words and Music by Ritchie Blackmore, Ian Gillan, Roger Glover, Jon Lord and Ian Paice

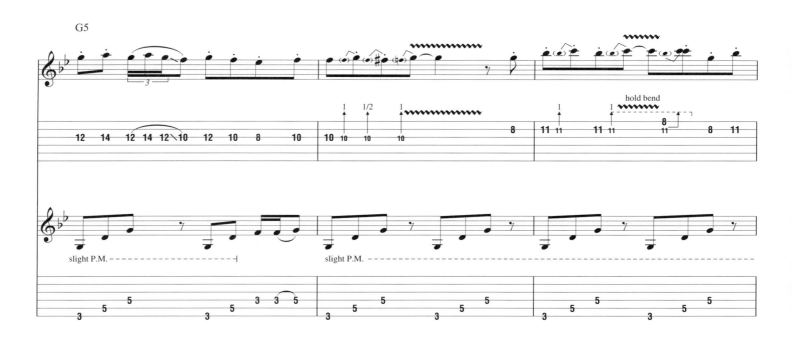

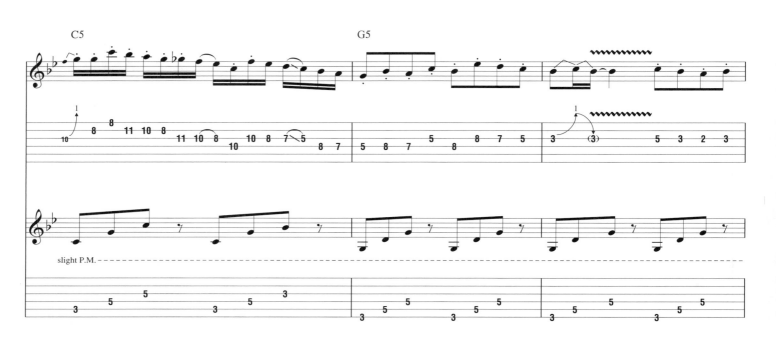

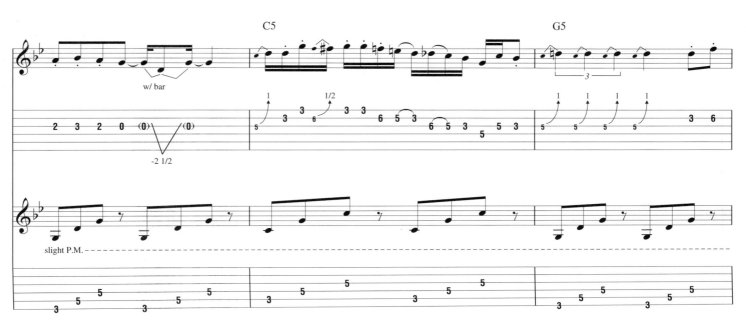

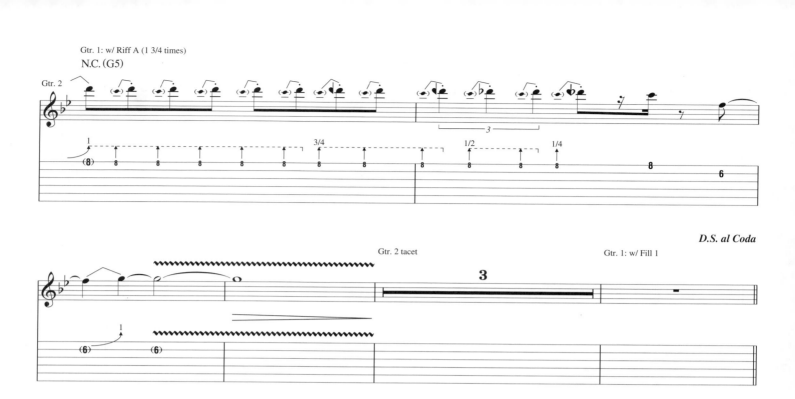

D.S. al Coda

Gtr. 2 tacet   Gtr. 1: w/ Fill 1

Coda

Interlude   **Outro-Organ Solo**

Begin fade

Fade out

Stellar

Words and Music by Brandon Boyd, Michael Einziger, Alex Katunich, Jose Pasillas II and Chris Kilmore

Chorus

How do you do __ it? __ Make me __ feel __ like __ I do. __

End Rhy. Fill 1   Rhy. Fig. 1

How do you do __ it? __ It's bet - ter __ than I ev - er knew, __

Interlude

oo. __

End Rhy. Fig. 1

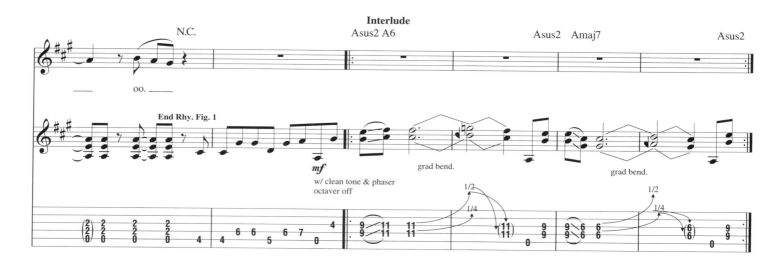

mf
w/ clean tone & phaser
octaver off

grad bend.   grad bend.

Verse

2. Meet __ me in out - er __ space. __

Riff B   **End Riff B**

phaser off

240

Gtr. 1: w/ Riff B (2 1/2 times)

I ___ will hold ___ you ___ close, ___ if you're a - fraid ___ of heights. I

need ___ you ___ to see ___ this ___ place, ___ it might be the on - ly way ___

Gtr. 1: w/ Rhy. Fill 1

that ___ I can show you ___ how ___ it feels ___ to be in - side ___

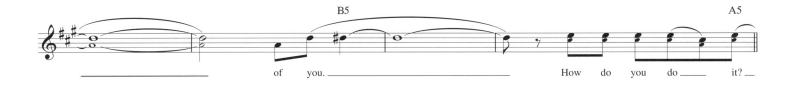

of you. ___ How do you do ___ it? ___

𝄋 Chorus

Gtr. 1: w/ Rhy. Fig. 1

___ Make me ___ feel ___ like ___ I do. ___ How do you do ___ it? ___

___ It's bet - ter ___ than I ev - er knew, ___ oo.

To Coda ⊕

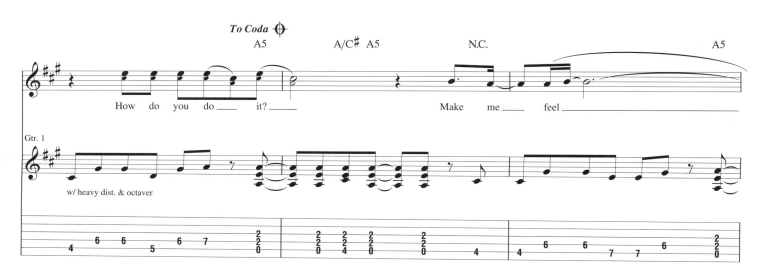

How do you do ___ it? ___ Make me ___ feel ___

Gtr. 1

w/ heavy dist. & octaver

Stop

Words and Music by Perry Farrell, Dave Navarro, Stephen Perkins and Eric Avery

G5

Intro
Free time

Spoken: Señores y señoras, nos otros de nemos mas influencia con sucijos que tu tiene. Pero los queremos. Creado y reado de Los Angeles, Juanes Adiccion.

*Chord symbols reflect overall harmony.

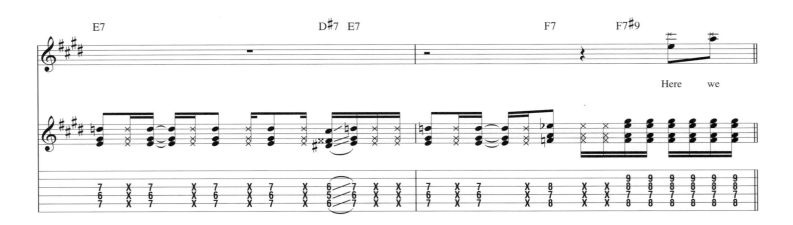

Here we

Chorus

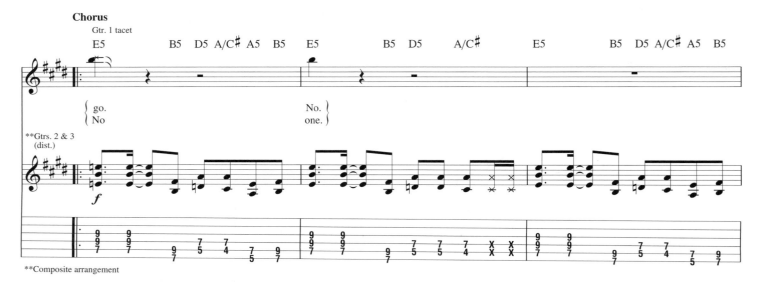

go. No.
No one.

**Gtr. 1 tacet

**Gtrs. 2 & 3 (dist.)

**Composite arrangement

244

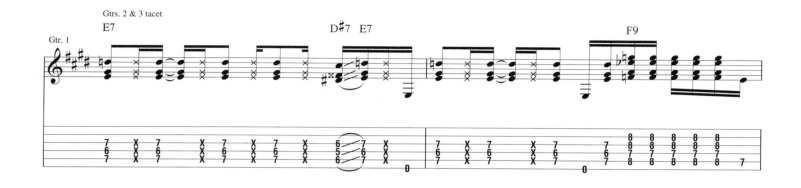

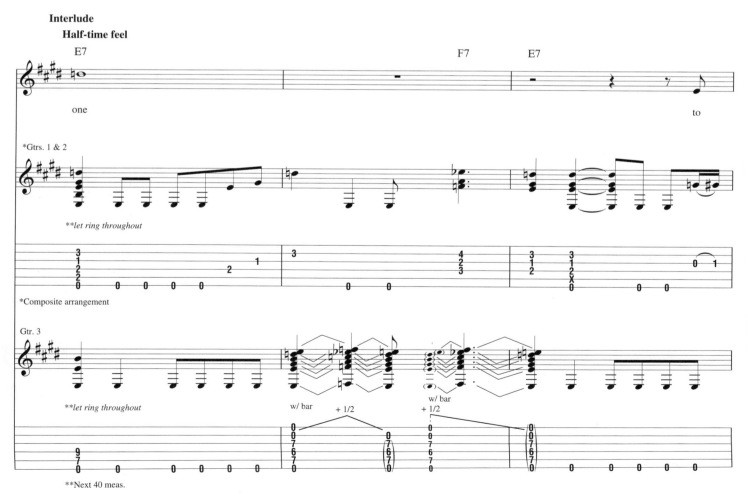

get con-trol of a mind like that. Move ___ on.

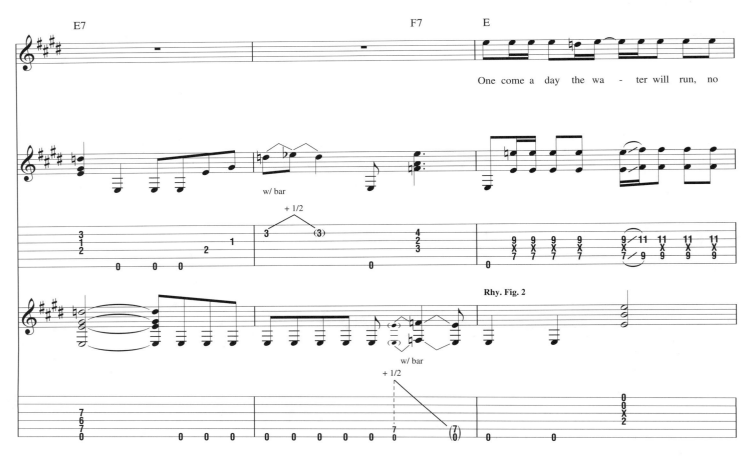

One come a day the wa - ter will run, no

man will stand for things that he had done. _____ Hur-

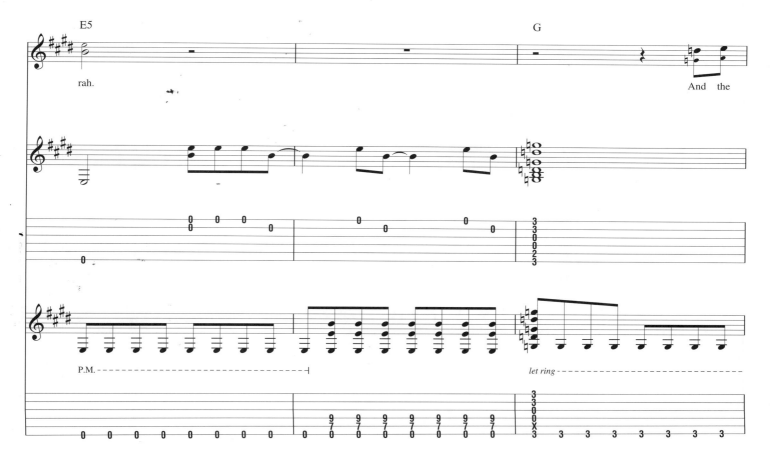

rah. And the

E5   G5

wa - ter will _ run.

Gtr. 3: w/ Rhy. Fig. 2

E5

One come a day_ the wa - ter will run, no   man will stand for things that   he   had

Gtrs. 1 & 2

End Rhy. Fig. 2

G5   E5

done. _   Hur - rah.

Gtrs. 1 & 2

Guitar Solo

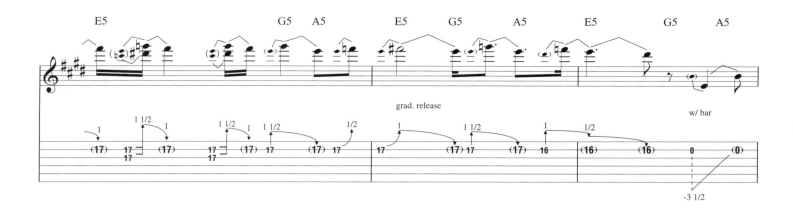

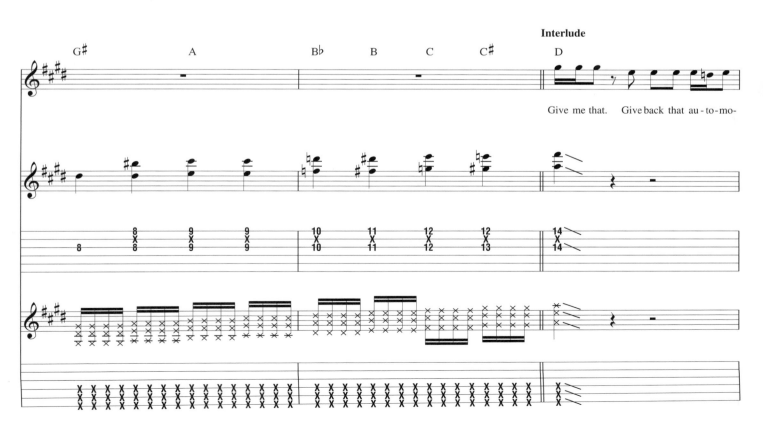

Give me that.   Give back that au-to-mo-

bile, turn off that smoke stack and that god - damn ra - di - o._____ Hum a - long with

me. Hum a - long with T V. Oh,_____ oh. Oh,_____

oh. Oh, oh,_____ oh._____ Oh,_____ no._____

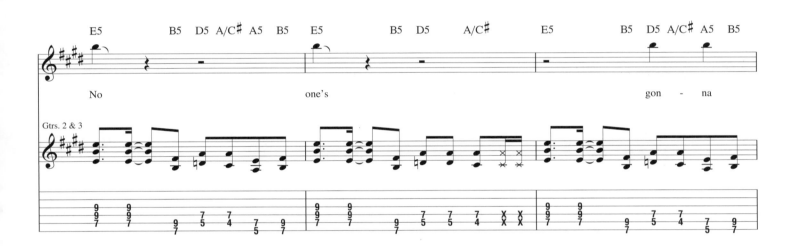

No one's gon - na

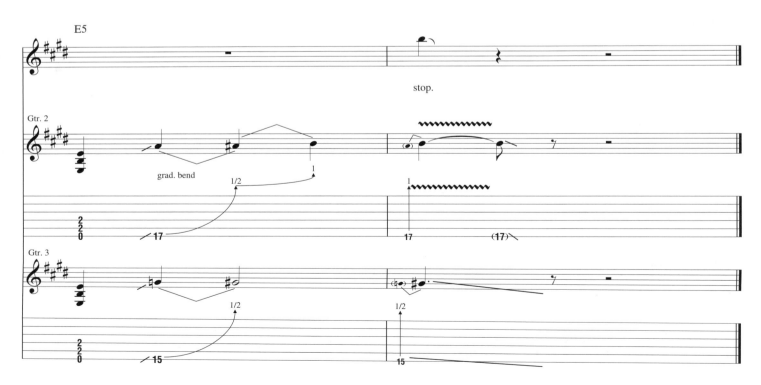

stop.

Strutter

Words and Music by Paul Stanley and Gene Simmons

Verse

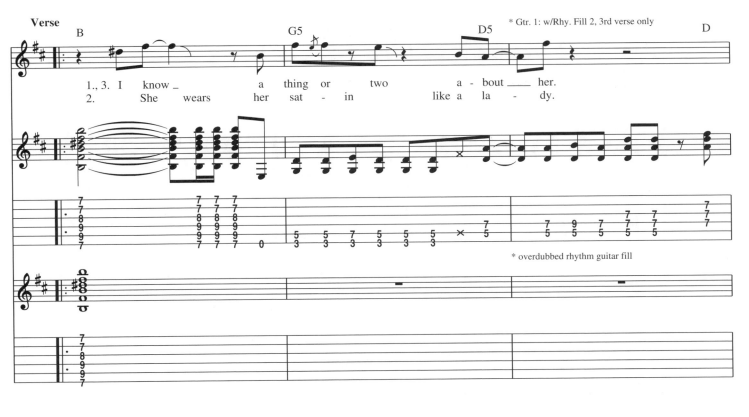

1., 3. I know __ a thing or two a-bout __ her.
2. She wears her sat-in like a la-dy.

* Gtr. 1: w/Rhy. Fill 2, 3rd verse only

* overdubbed rhythm guitar fill

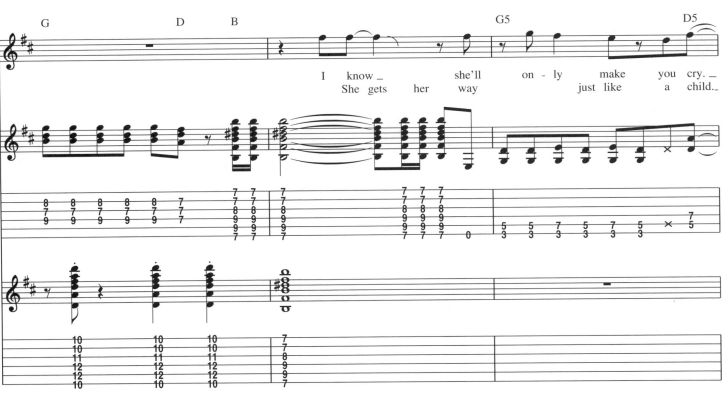

I know __ she'll on-ly make you cry. __
She gets her way just like a child.__

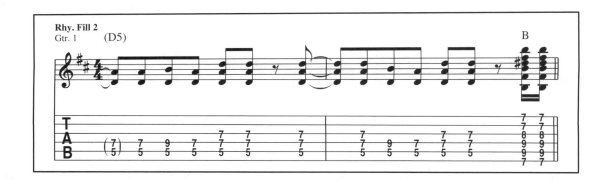

Rhy. Fill 2
Gtr. 1   (D5)

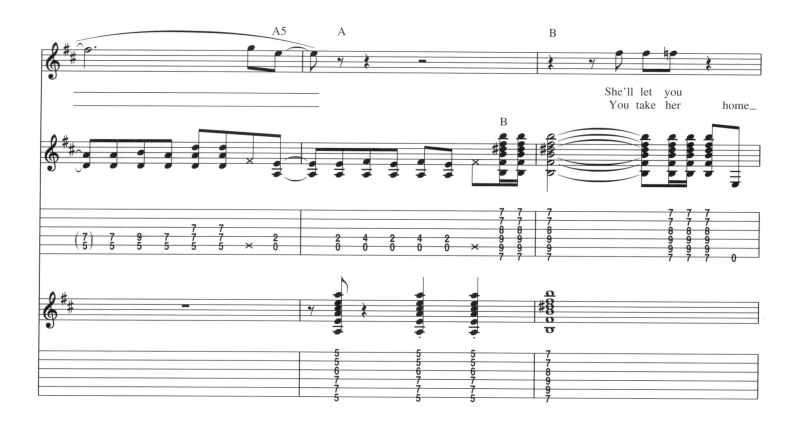

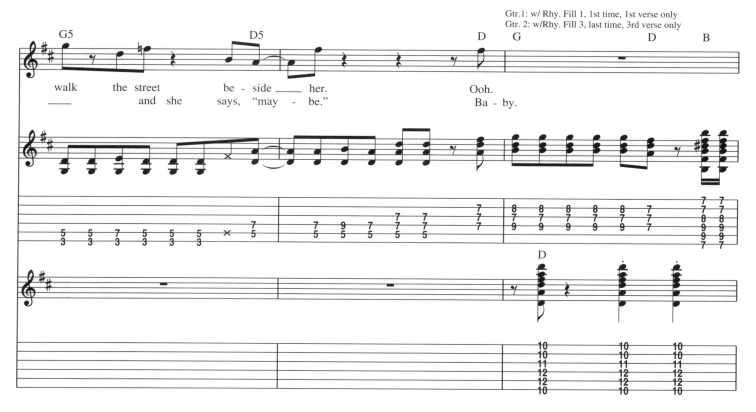

Gtr.1: w/ Rhy. Fill 1, 1st time, 1st verse only
Gtr. 2: w/Rhy. Fill 3, last time, 3rd verse only

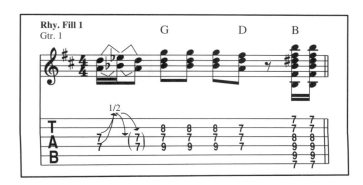

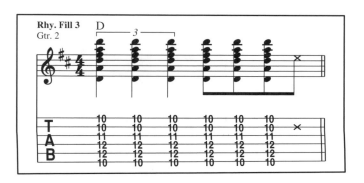

and the la - dy knows it's un - der - stood.____ Strut - ter.

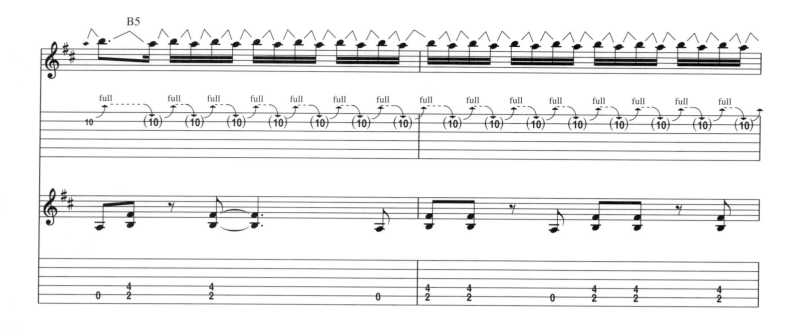

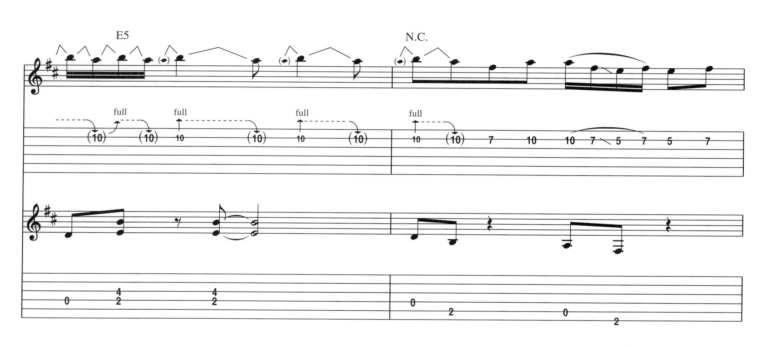

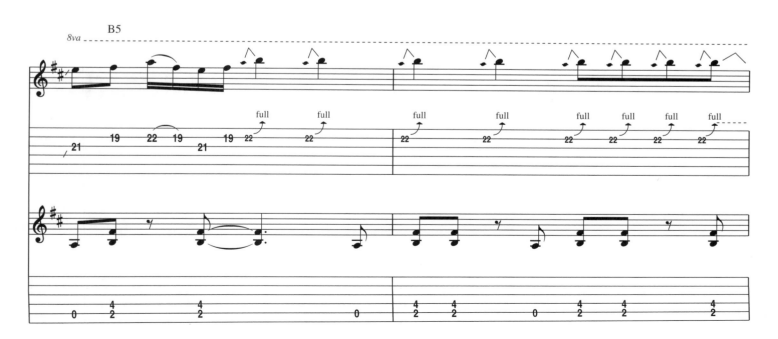

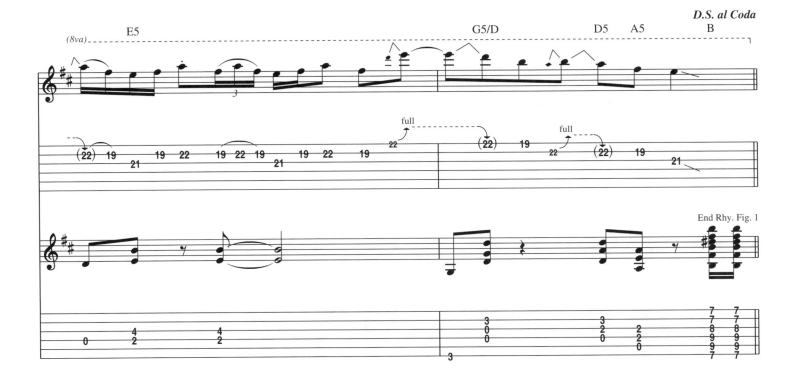

⊕ *Coda*

Outro

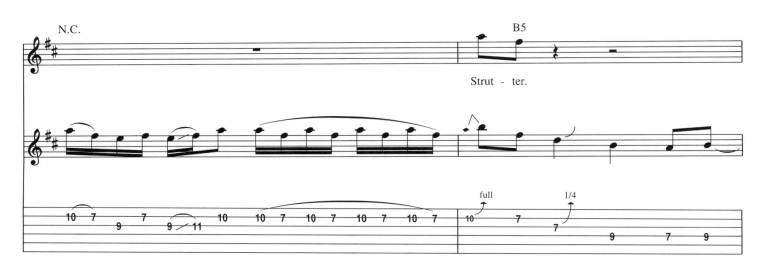

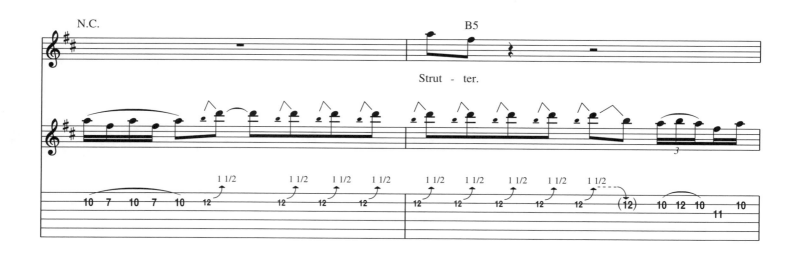

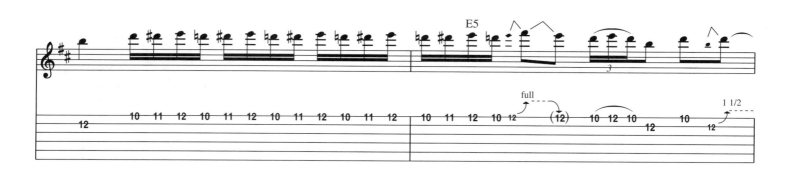

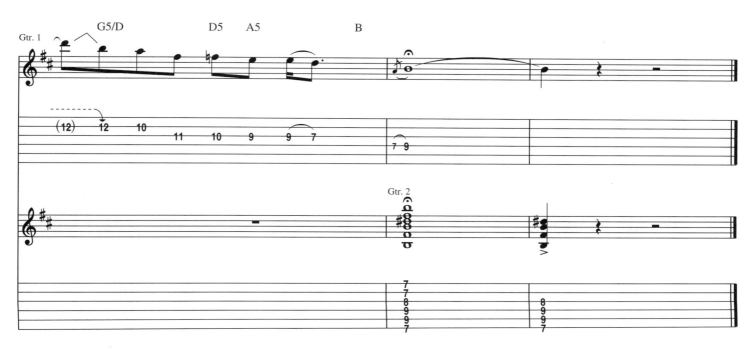

Surrender

Words and Music by Rick Nielsen

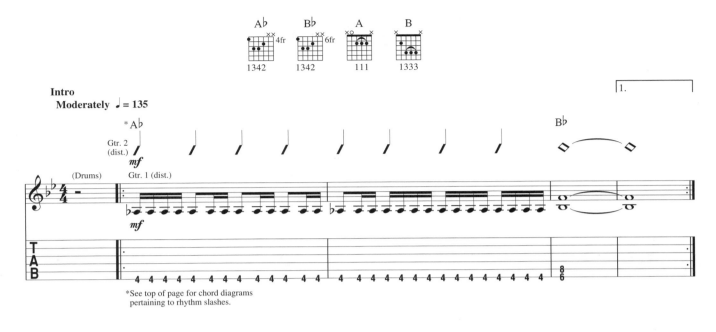

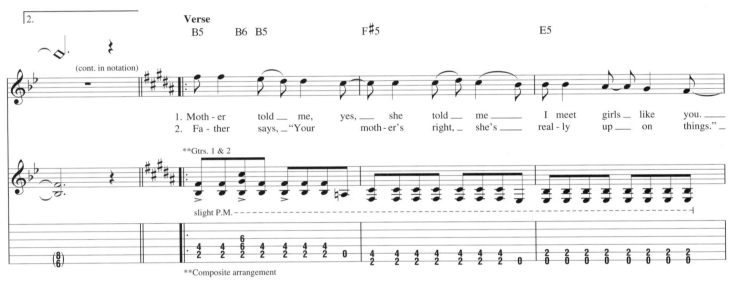

*See top of page for chord diagrams
pertaining to rhythm slashes.

**Composite arrangement

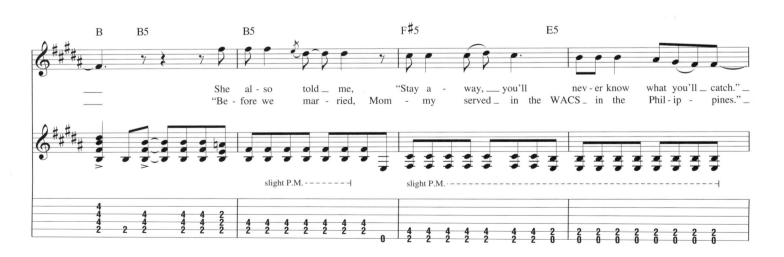

1. Moth-er told me, yes, she told me I meet girls like you.
2. Fa-ther says, "Your moth-er's right, she's real-ly up on things."

She al-so told me, "Stay a-way, you'll nev-er know what you'll catch."
"Be-fore we mar-ried, Mom-my served in the WACS in the Phil-ip-pines."

Pre-Chorus

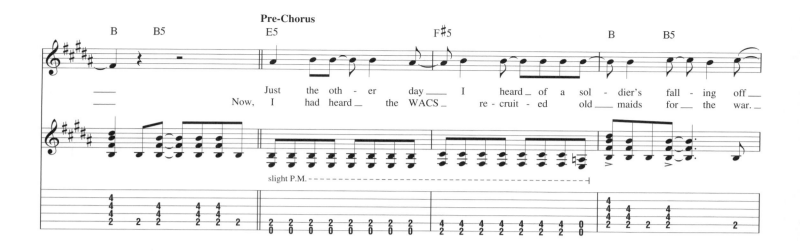

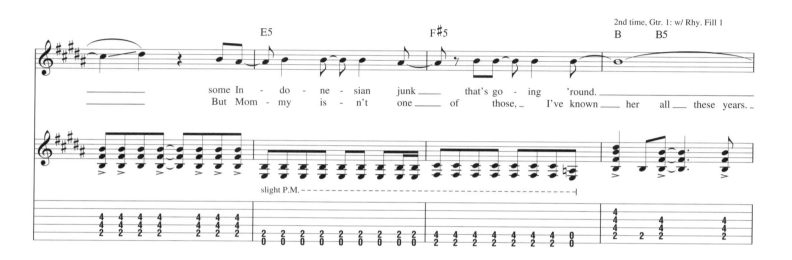

Chorus

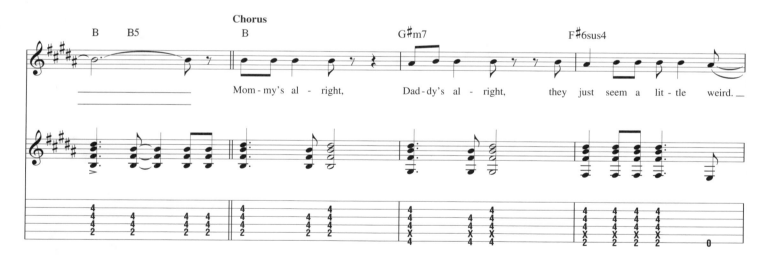

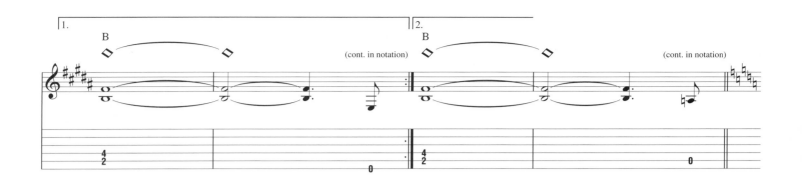

Verse

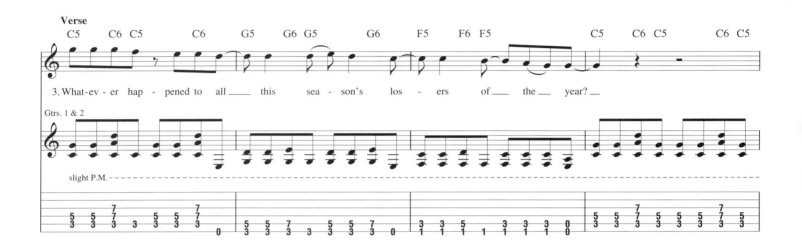

3. What-ev - er hap - pened to all ___ this sea - son's los - ers of ___ the ___ year? ___

Gtrs. 1 & 2

slight P.M. ---

Ev-'ry - time ___ I got ___ to think - in', where'd they dis - ap - pear? ___

slight P.M. -- P.M. --

Pre-Chorus

Then I woke ___ up, Mom and Dad ___ are roll - in' on ___ the couch. ___

P.M. -- slight P.M. -

Bridge

*Refers to Bkgd. Voc. only, sung **mp**.

Outro-Chorus

Sweet Child o' Mine

Words and Music by W. Axl Rose, Slash, Izzy Stradlin', Duff McKagan and Steven Adler

271

Oh,   oh, __ oh,   oh, _____ sweet   child _ o' mine. _____

Woo, __ yeah, _ yeah!   Ooh, _____ sweet love o' mine. _____

Guitar Solo

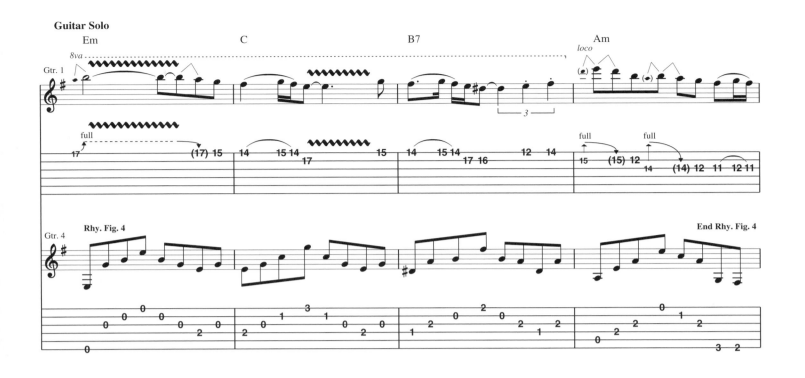

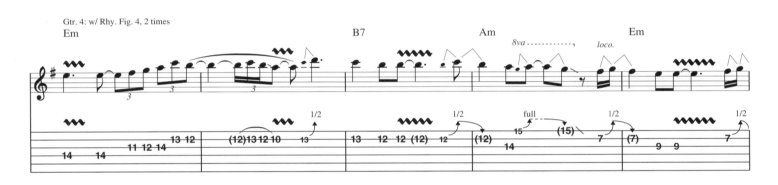

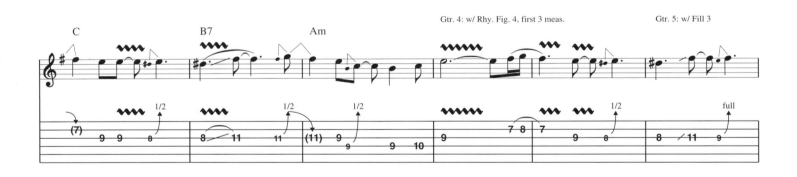

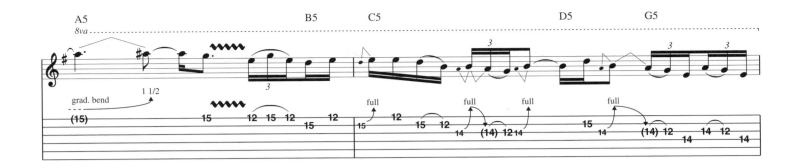

Gtr. 2: w/ Rhy. Fig. 6, 2 times

Where do we go? _ Where do we go _ now? Where do we go? _ Where do we go? _

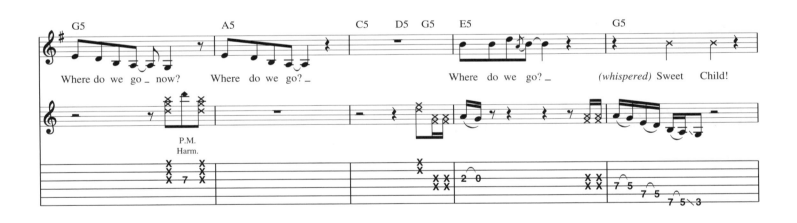

Where do we go _ now? Where do we go? _ Where do we go? _ (whispered) Sweet Child!

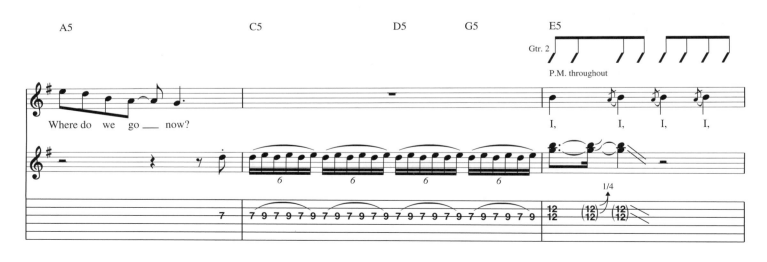

Where do we go ___ now? I, I, I, I,

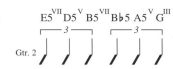

Gtr. 2: w/ Rhy. Fig. 7, first 3 meas.

E5   G5   A5   B5   E5^{VII} D5^V B5^{VII} B♭5 A5^V G^{III}

Where do we go? _____   Where do we go _ now?   No, no, no, no, no, no,

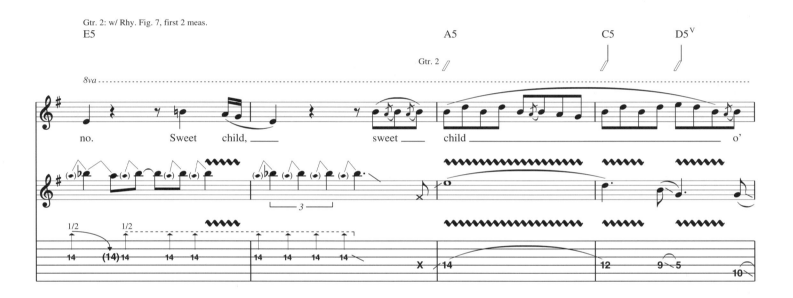

Gtr. 2: w/ Rhy. Fig. 7, first 2 meas.

E5   A5   C5   D5^V

no.   Sweet   child, _____   sweet _____ child _____ o'

E5

mine. _____

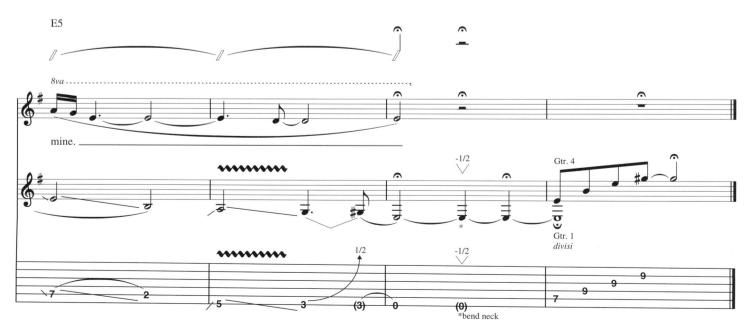

277

Symphony of Destruction

Words and Music by Dave Mustaine

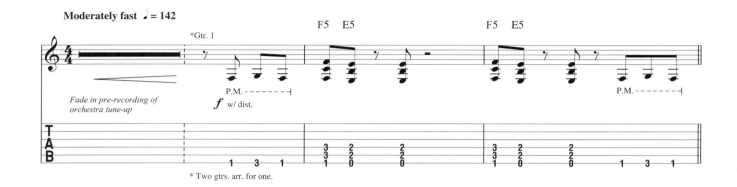

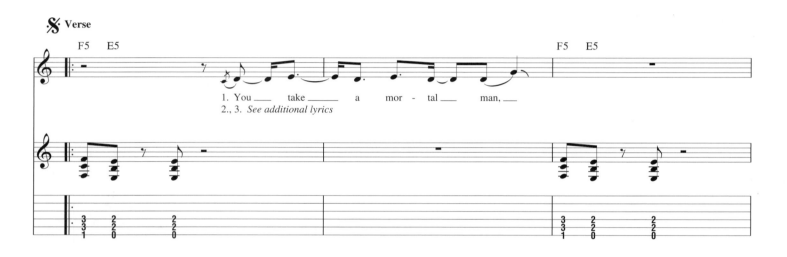

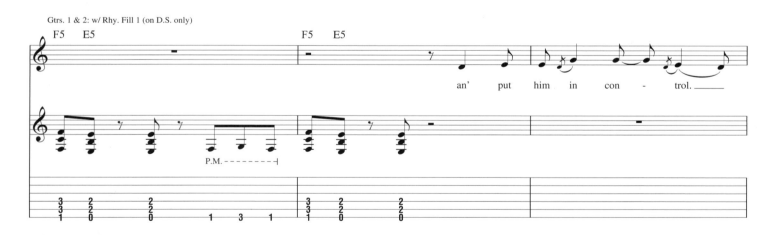

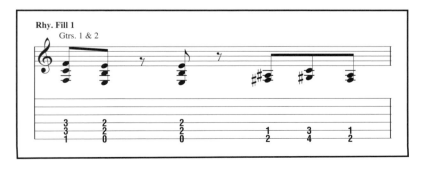

Chorus

Just like the Pied _____ Pip - er led _____ rats

through _____ the streets. We dance like the mar - i - on - ettes,

sway-in' _____ to the Sym - pho - ny of De - struc - tion. _____

Sym- pho- ny. Just like the Pied _____ Pip - er

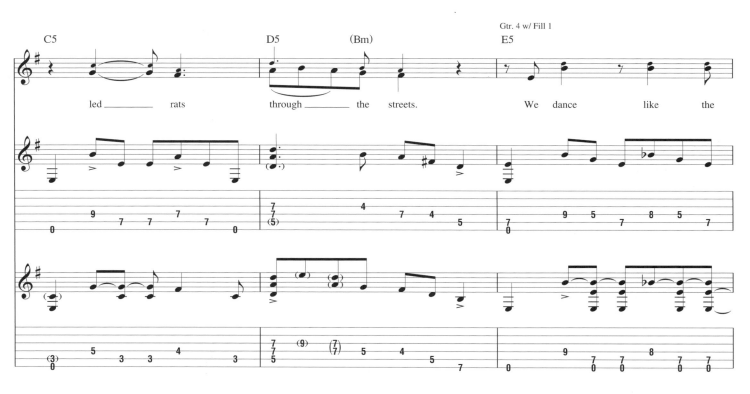

led _____ rats through _____ the streets. We dance like the

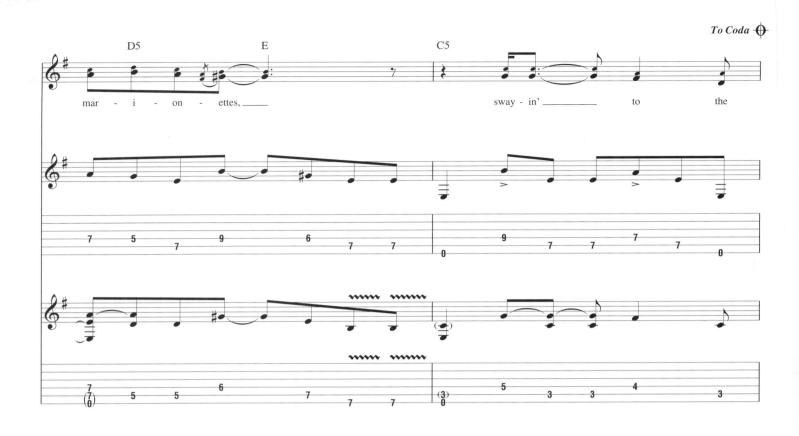

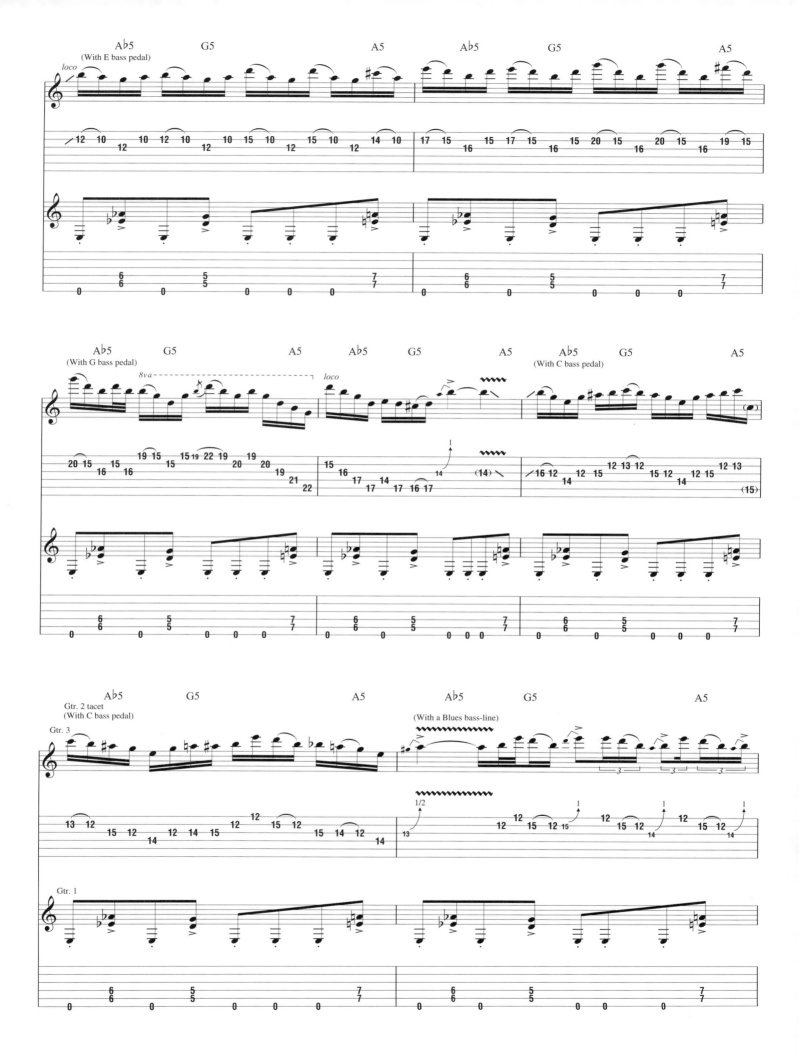

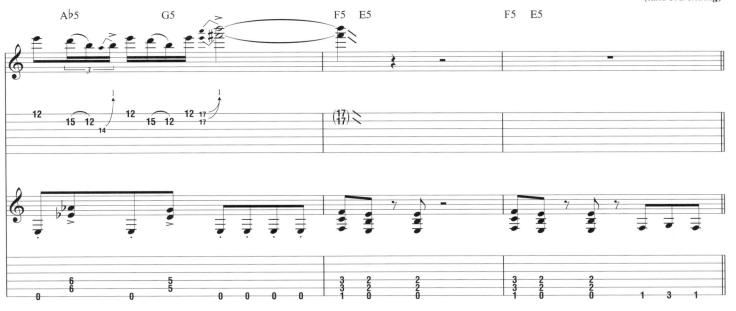

Additional Lyrics

2. Acting like a robot
   It's metal brain corrodes
   Try to take it's pulse
   Before the head explodes, explodes, explodes, ah...

3. The earth starts to rumble
   World powers fall
   Warring for the heavens
   A peaceful man stands tall, tall, tall...

Texas Flood

Words and Music by Larry Davis and Joseph W. Scott

Well, _____ it's _____ flood-in' down _ in Tex-as. _____

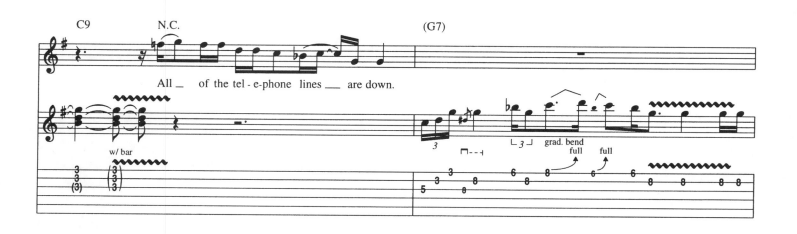

All _ of the tel - e-phone lines _____ are down.

Yeah, _____ I been try-in' to call _____ my ba - by. _____

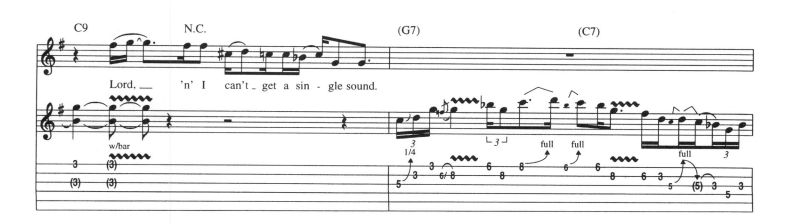

Lord, _____ 'n' I can't _ get a sin - gle sound.

Yeah, _____ flood _____ wa-ter keep a-roll - in',

man, it's a-bout to drive poor me in-sane. _____

Guitar Solo

3. Well, ___ I'm

Verse

leav-in' you ba-by. _____

Lord, ___ now I'm go-in' back home ___ to stay.

Well, _____ I'm ___ leav-in' you ba - by. _____

Lord, _____ 'n' I'm go-in' back home to stay.

Well, _ back home there's no _ floods or tor - na - does,

babe, _____ 'n' the _ sun shines _ ev - 'ry day. _____

Free Time

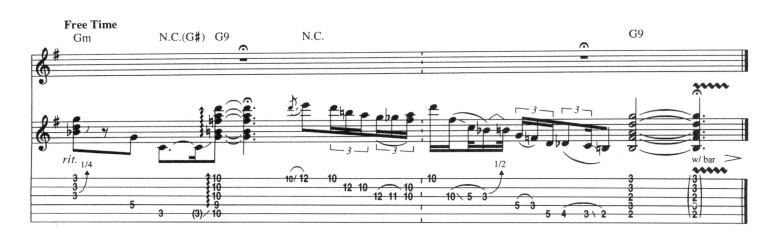

Them Bones

Written by Jerry Cantrell

Tune down 1/2 step
Tune low E down 1 1/2 steps

⑥=D♭ ③=G♭

⑤=A♭ ②=B♭

④=D♭ ①=E♭

The Trooper

Words and Music by Steven Harris

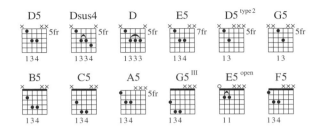

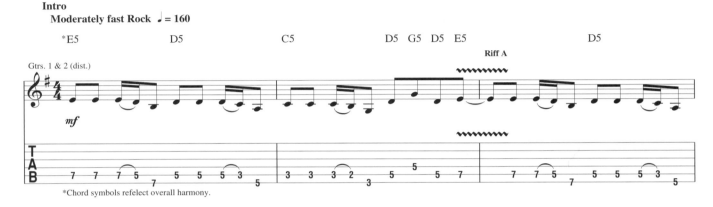

*Chord symbols relfect overall harmony.

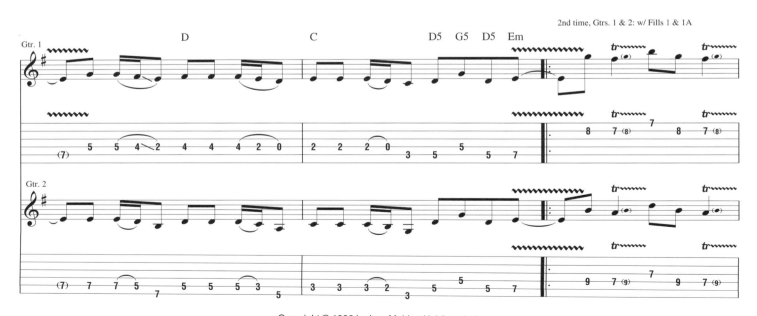

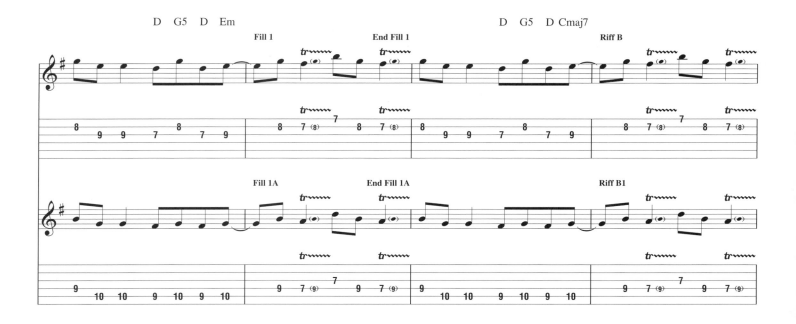

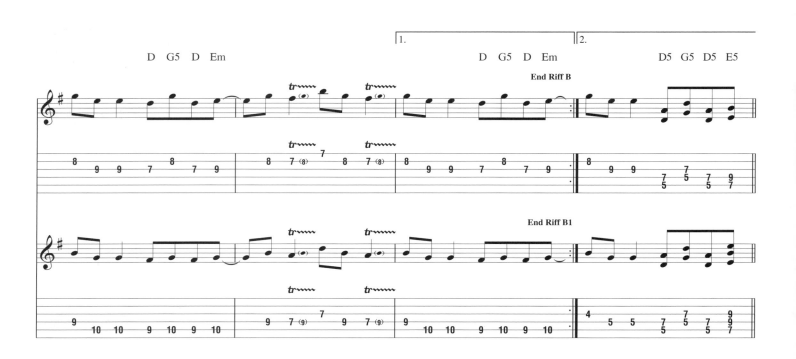

1. You'll take my life but I'll take yours too. ___ You'll fire your mus-ket but I'll
2. The horse, he sweats with fear; we break to run. ___ The might-y roar of the
3. We got so close, near e-nough to fight. ___ When a Rus-sian gets me

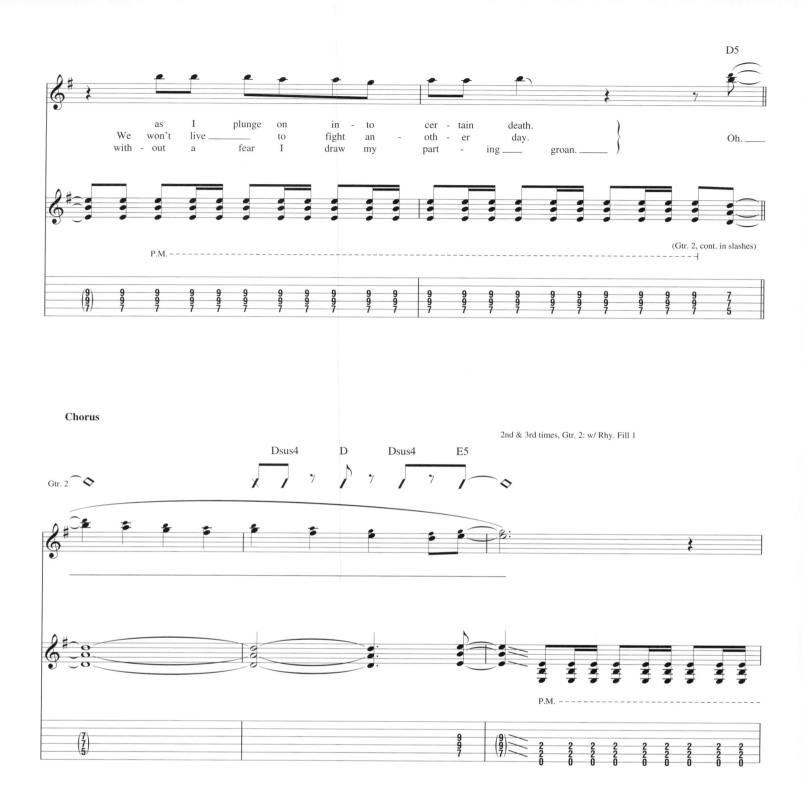

D5

We | as | I | plunge | on | in | - | to | cer | - | tain | death.
won't | live _____ | to | fight | an | - | oth | - | er | day.
with | - | out | a | fear | I | draw | my | part | - | ing _____ | groan. _____

Oh. _____

(Gtr. 2, cont. in slashes)

P.M. -

Chorus

2nd & 3rd times, Gtr. 2: w/ Rhy. Fill 1

Dsus4   D   Dsus4   E5

Gtr. 2

P.M. - - - - - - -

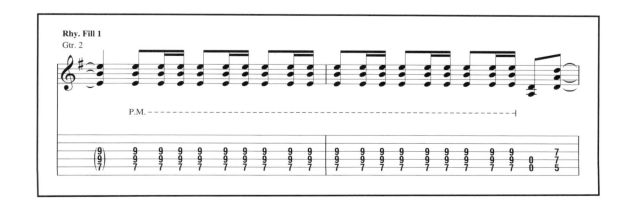

Rhy. Fill 1
Gtr. 2

P.M. -

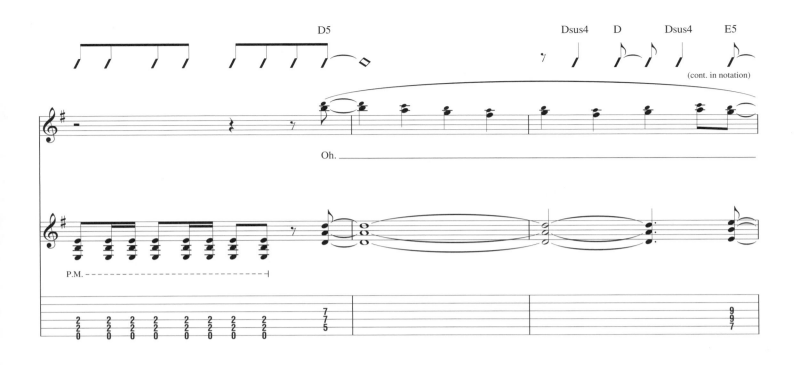

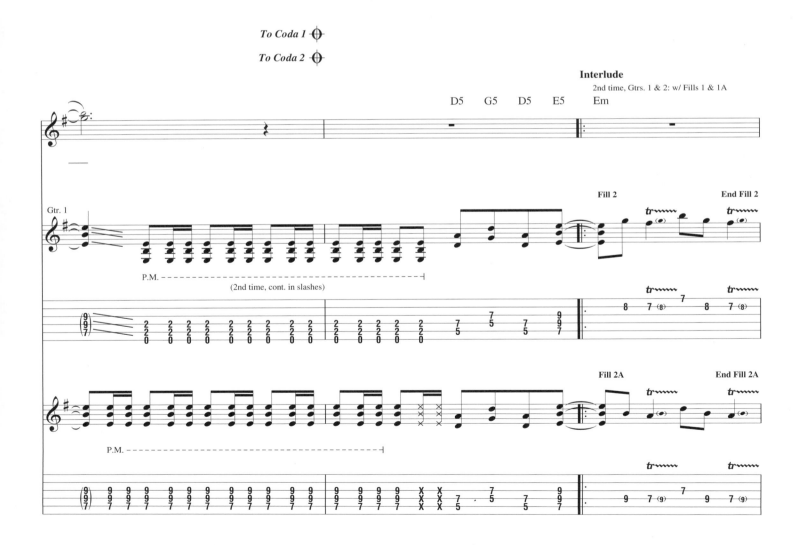

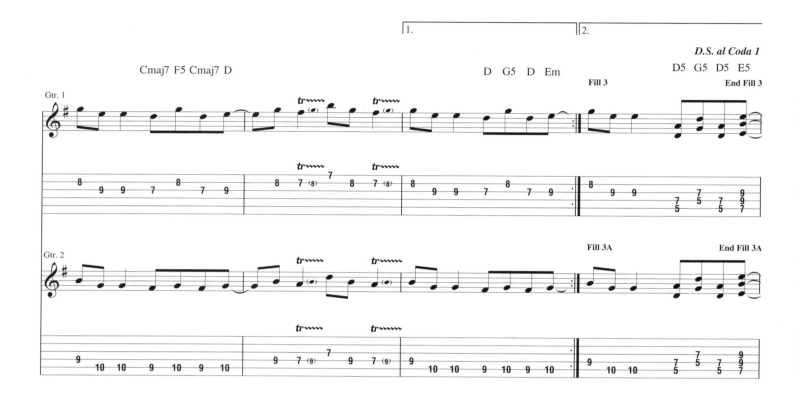

 Coda 1

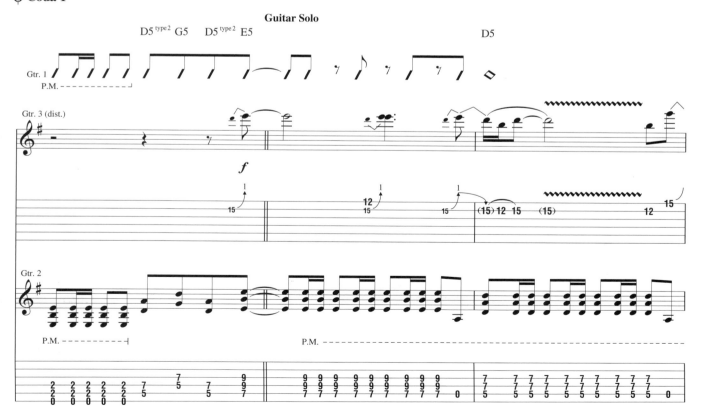

303

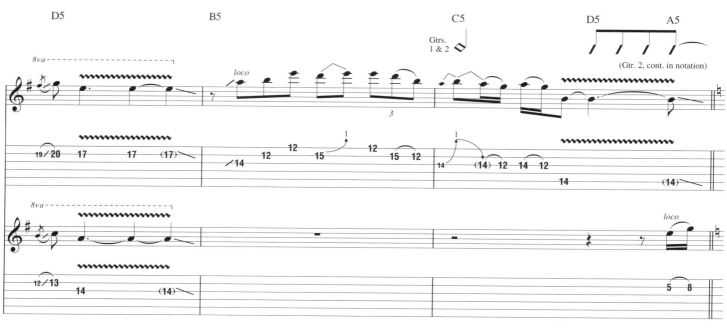

Guitar Solo

Gtr. 3 tacet

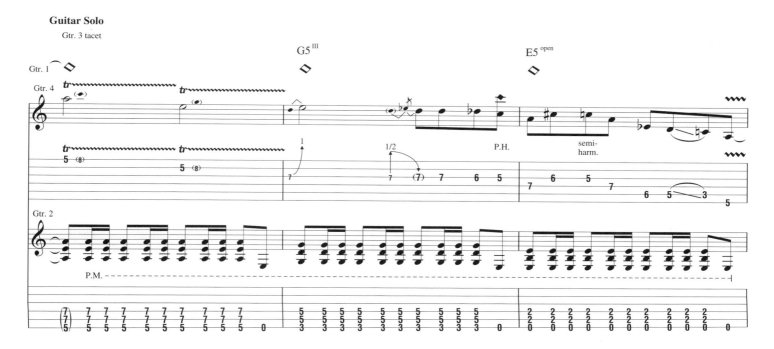

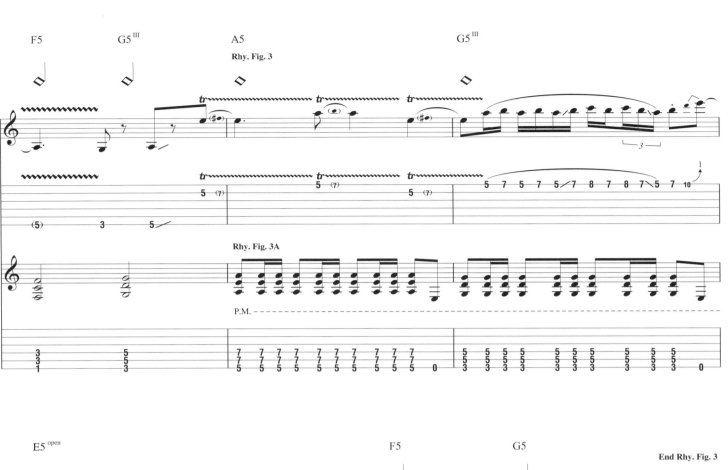

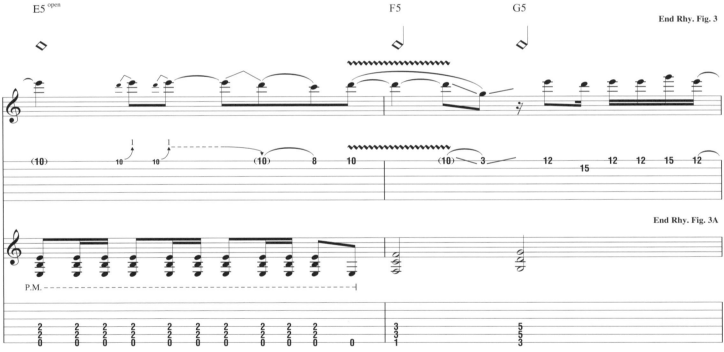

Gtrs. 1 & 2: w/ Rhy. Figs. 3 & 3A (1 1/4 times)

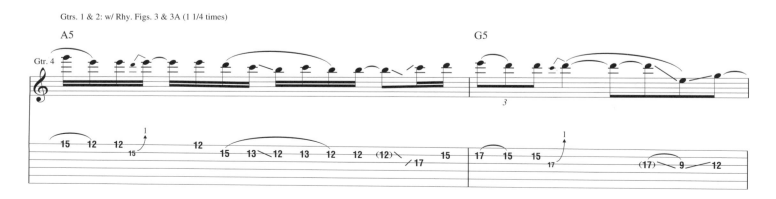

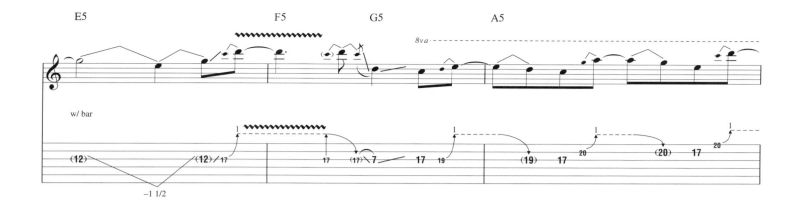

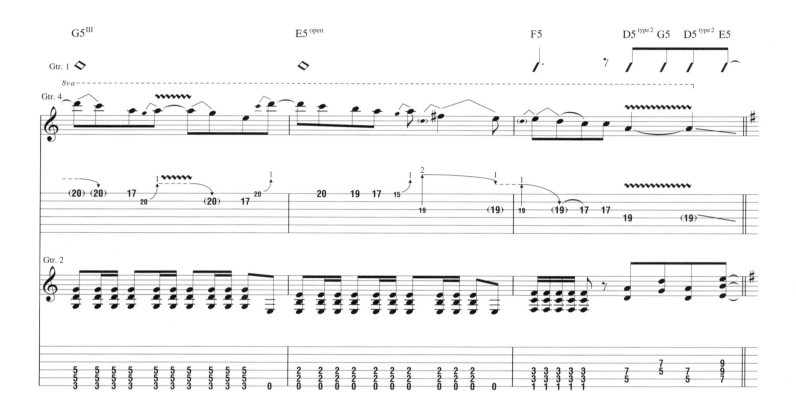

Interlude

1st time, Gtrs. 1 & 2: w/ Fills 2 & 2A
1st time, Gtr. 4 tacet
2nd time, Gtrs. 1 & 2: w/ Fills 1 & 1A

Gtrs. 1 & 2: w/ Riffs B & B1 (last 3 meas.)

1st time, Gtrs. 1 & 2: w/ Riffs B & B1
2nd time, Gtrs. 1 & 2: w/ Riffs B & B1 (1st 3 meas.)

D.S. al Coda 2

Gtrs. 1 & 2: w/ Fills 3 & 3A

Coda 2

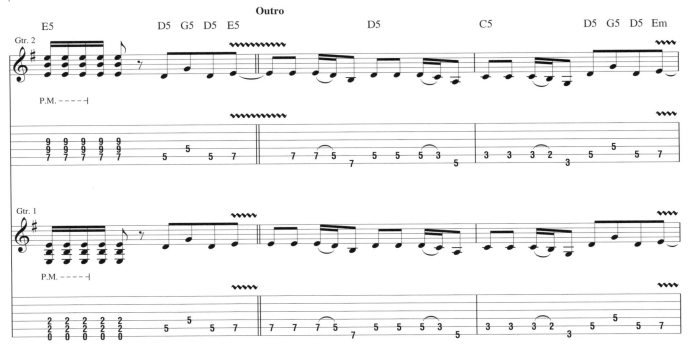

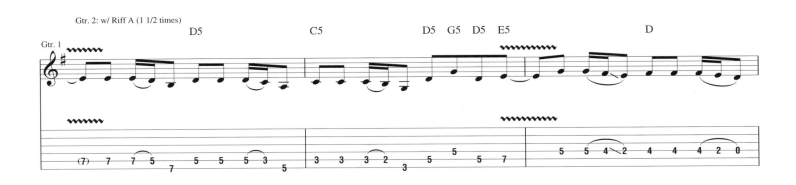

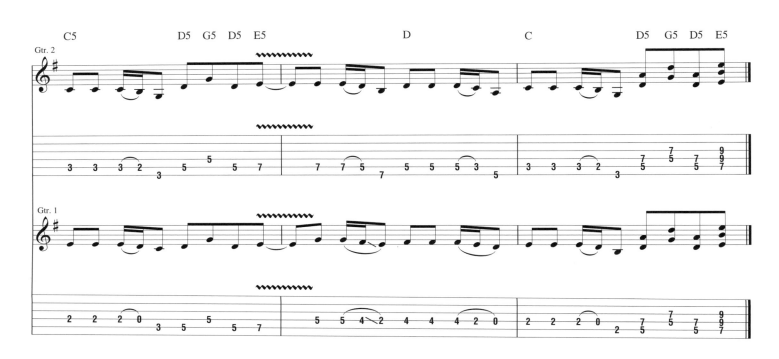

You Really Got Me

Words and Music by Ray Davies

Tune Down 1/2 Step:
(low to high) E♭-B♭-G♭-D♭-A♭-E♭

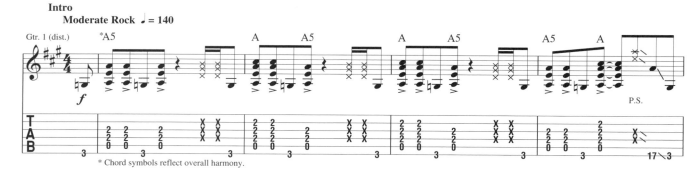

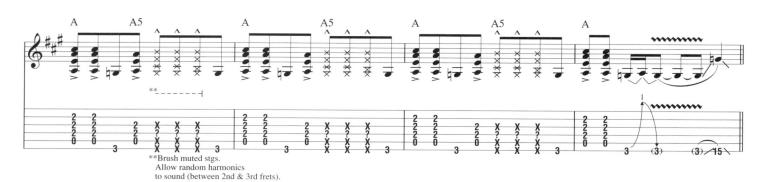

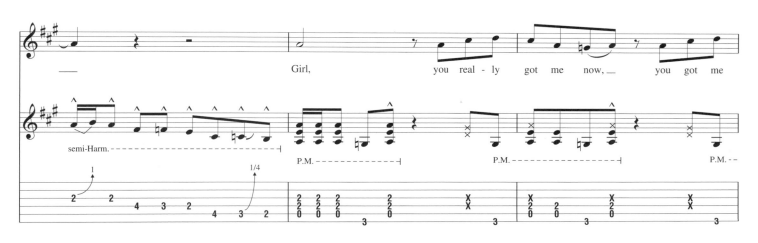

You've Got Another Thing Comin'

Words and Music by Glenn Tipton, Rob Halford and K.K. Downing

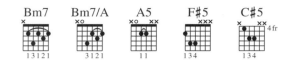

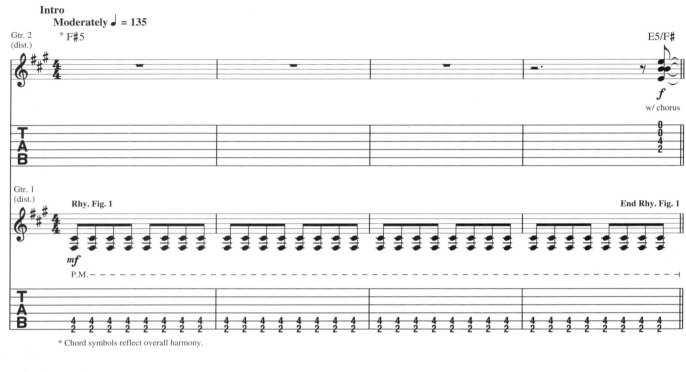

* Chord symbols reflect overall harmony.

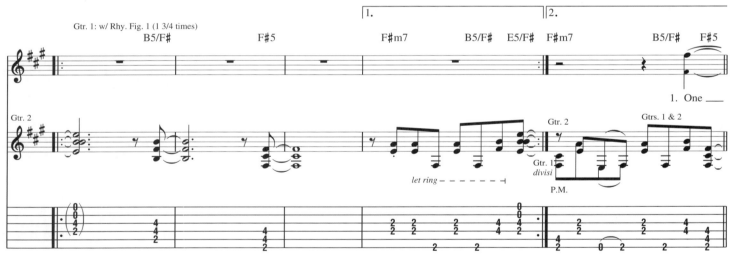

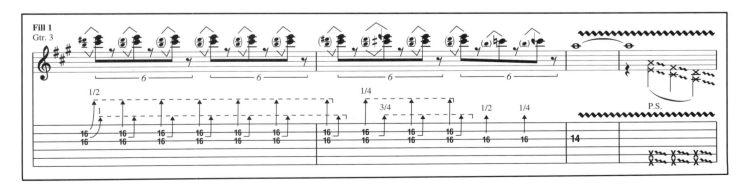

Guitar Solo

Gtrs. 1 & 2: w/ Rhy. Fig. 4, 1st 2 meas. (4 times)

318

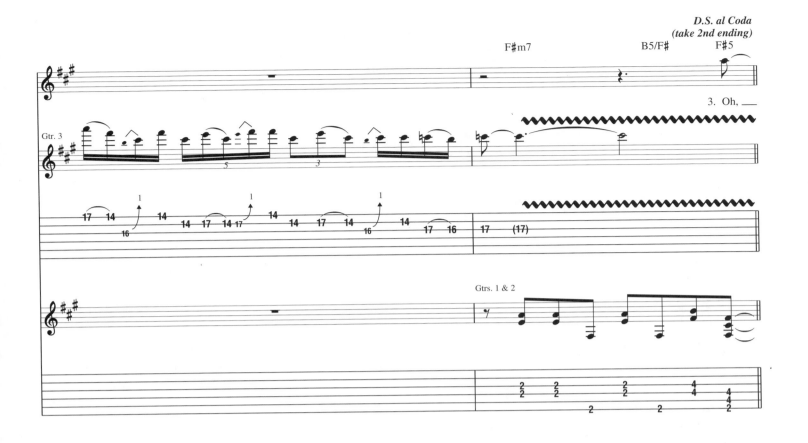

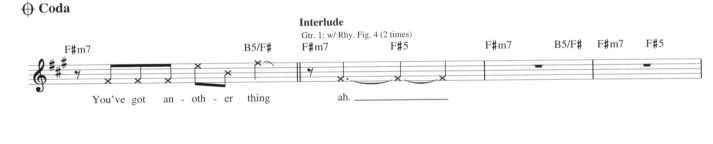

⊕ Coda

Interlude
Gtr. 1: w/ Rhy. Fig. 4 (2 times)

You've got an - oth - er thing ah. ____

Com - in' on down!

Play 10 times and fade

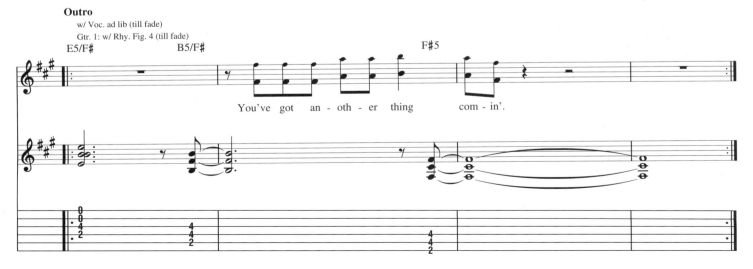

Outro
w/ Voc. ad lib (till fade)
Gtr. 1: w/ Rhy. Fig. 4 (till fade)

You've got an - oth - er thing com - in'.

Ziggy Stardust

Words and Music by David Bowie

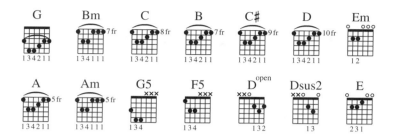

* Chord symbols reflect basic harmony.

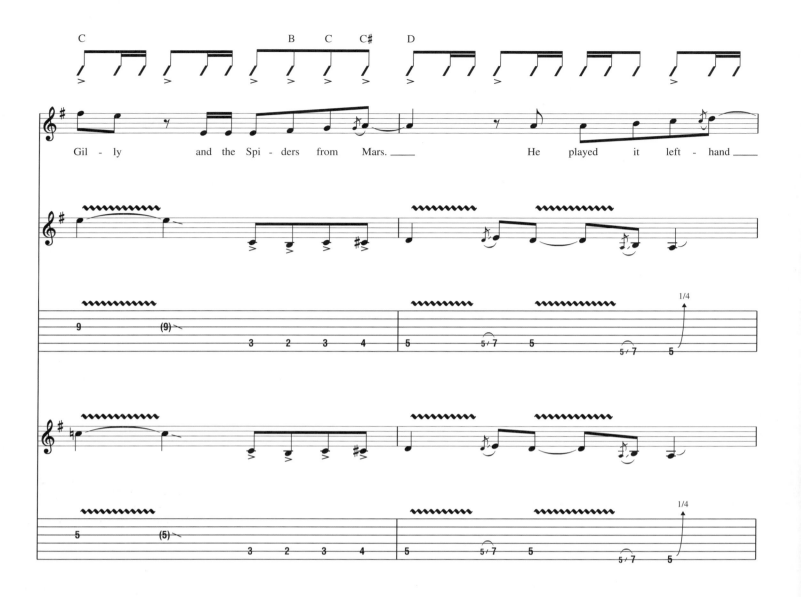

Gil - ly and the Spi - ders from Mars. ___ He played it left - hand ___

*Gtrs. 1 & 4

Gtr. 1

Gtr. 4 tacet

Harm. ------

fdbk.

but made it too far. ___ Be - came _ the spec - ial man. _ A, then we were

* Composite arrangement

pitch: E

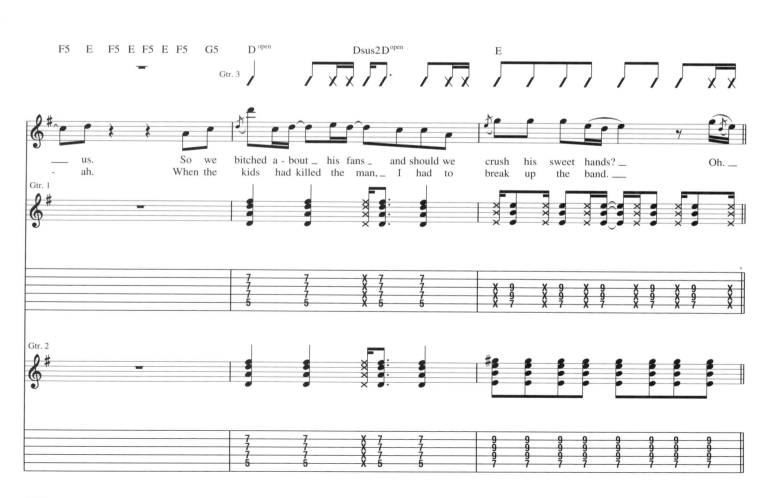